DECISION SUPPORT SYSTEMS

DECISION SUPPORT SYSTEMS

Proceedings of the NYU Symposium on Decision Support Systems
New York, 21-22 May, 1981

edited by

Michael J. GINZBERG

Walter REITMAN

and

Edward A. STOHR

Computer Applications and
Informations Systems,
Graduate School of Business Administration,
New York University

1982

NORTH-HOLLAND PUBLISHING COMPANY
AMSTERDAM · NEW YORK · OXFORD

cc.

ISBN: 0 444 86472 5

Publisher:

NORTH-HOLLAND PUBLISHING COMPANY
AMSTERDAM · NEW YORK · OXFORD

Sole distributors for the U.S.A. and Canada:

ELSEVIER SCIENCE PUBLISHING COMPANY, INC.
52 VANDERBILT AVENUE
NEW YORK, N.Y. 10017

Printed in the Netherlands

PREFACE

This book contains the papers presented at the 1981 NYU Symposium on Decision Support Systems. The Symposium was sponsored by the Affiliates Program of the NYU Center for Research on Information Systems, and we want to thank the members of the Program for their support. We also want to thank our colleagues in the Computer Applications and Information Systems Department who provided advice and encouragement throughout this project. We are indebted to the authors of the papers for their continued cooperation, to Jesse Tigner-Hayden for producing the final manuscript, and especially to Carole Larson, who always came through when we needed her.

M.J.G.
W.R.
E.A.S.

New York City
May 1982

TABLE OF CONTENTS

INTRODUCTION

The purpose of the NYU Symposium on Decision Support Systems (DSS) was to bring together researchers and practitioners interested in DSS in order to assess where the field stands and where it is heading. DSS has emerged as a topic of great interest to computer users, business managers, academic researchers, and computer industry vendors within the past several years. It has replaced MIS as the "hot" application area for computers in business.

While the degree of interest in DSS is clear, the DSS concept itself (like the MIS concept before it) is not so clear. DSS is a field or an area of interest which attempts to bring together and focus a number of independent disciplines. Among these are:

1. Operations Research/Management Science. These disciplines are the traditional home of people concerned with model building and the application of mathematical techniques to business problems. The great majority of DSS incorporate some sort of model, and as these models become more sophisticated, the skills and knowledge of OR/MS specialists become necessary to guild these systems. On the other hand, most practical applications of OR/MS require both large amounts of data and considerable computation, and thus must be computer based. As a result, an increasing number of OR/MS specialists find themselves developing computer-based models and modeling systems. They are providing computer-based support for managerial decision making, i.e., DSS.

2. Data-base technology. The data base discipline has been concerned with the development of tools to collect, store, and retrieve large volumes of diverse data. These tools are meant to be general purpose, and are not designed for any specific application context. DSS often incorporate large amounts of data, and these systems—like many others—require some mechanism to manage the data they use. Data-base management systems are a logical candidate for this role, and are frequently found as a component of DSS.

3. Artificial intelligence. Artificial intelligence (AI) is a discipline which attempts to build software systems exhibiting near-human "intellectual" capabilities. Much work in AI has focused on such tasks as natural language comprehension, theorem proving, and symbolic algebra problem solution. While these tasks are not directly relevant to DSS, many researchers believe that the next generation of DSS will have to incorporate techniques developed for AI systems.

4. Systems engineering. Data processing professionals have developed, during the 20 or more years that computers have been used in organizations, numerous techniques for system analysis, design and implementation. For the most part, these techniques were developed to meet the needs presented by large scale transaction processing systems. DSS, too, must be analyzed, designed, and implemented, though the techniques required may differ from those used in the past.

1

5. **Decision analysis.** This discipline can be divided into two major areas. The first, descriptive analysis, is concerned with understanding how people actually make decisions. The second, normative analysis, attempts to prescribe how people should make decisions. Both are issues of concern to DSS; the central aim of this field is improving the decision making process, but improvement is only possible if it is practical. Thus, the prescriptions of a normative analysis must be tempered by the realities which a descriptive analysis will show.

What brings these diverse disciplines together into the field called DSS is an interest in affecting decision making in organizations. DSS, is an attempt to integrate these independent disciplines, to bring their separate technologies to bear on decision making in organizations. Such integration, of course, is not easy. Most players in the DSS game are interested primarily in only one aspect of the overall problem, that aspect represented by their "home discipline." Thus, much of the DSS literature has a particular slant — e.g., requirements analysis techniques for DSS, use of data base techniques in DSS, etc. — and does not present an integrated view of DSS.

The participants in the NYU Symposium represent all factions of the DSS community: from practitioners to theoretical researchers, from technologists to behaviorists. Their individual contributions (like most of the DSS literature) represent their own special sub-interests, but taken together they present a reasonably comprehensive view of current thinking about DSS. We believe that this volume has something to offer a wide range of readers. To the DSS novice, the person just coming to the field, it offers a broad introduction. For the DSS practitioner it provides detailed examples of current systems, recent findings about the DSS development process, as well as an introduction to the technologies which are likely to play an important role in future DSS. To the DSS user it offers several examples of innovative DSS applications and provides guidance on appropriate user roles in DSS development. Finally, for the DSS researcher, it suggests areas where further research work is needed if the field is to advance. In the remainder of this introduction we shall preview the 8 papers in this volume, attempting to show what each has to offer to each type of reader.

DECISION SUPPORT SYSTEMS: ISSUES AND PERSPECTIVES

The paper by Ginzberg and Stohr attempts to define and provide an orientation to the DSS field. They note that a number of non-intersecting definitions of DSS have been offered in recent years, and that each definition represents the special interest (e.g., home discipline) of the author proposing it. They argue that the definition of DSS must reflect the central concern of the *DSS* field, i.e., the support and improvement of decision making in organizations.

Following the discussion of DSS definitions, the paper provides an extensive discussion of the components from which DSS are built, the ways in which DSS are used, and the processes by which they are developed. In each case, the discussion focuses on how DSS differ from other types of computer-based systems, as well as the differences which can be observed across DSS.

This paper provides a general introduction to DSS which attempts to synthesize and reconcile the apparently conflicting points of view represented in previous DSS literature. The discussion of DSS components, usage, and development patterns should be particularly useful, as it will help readers in assessing how well their existing resources equip them for DSS development efforts. Researchers should find the substantial bibliography of DSS literature and the numerous suggestions for further research quite helpful.

THE INTEGRATION OF BUSINESS INFORMATION SYSTEMS FOR DECISION SUPPORT SYSTEMS IN APL

Mattern's paper begins by noting the gap that often exists between an organization's transaction processing systems and the needs of managers for information relevant to decision making. He argues that the APL language — because of its concise and powerful operators, its interpretative nature, and the speed with which new applications can be developed using it — is a tool which can help to bridge that gap. To bolster his argument he points out that the majority of the application experience with APL has been in developing DSS, and the great bulk (90%) of internal computer usage by IBM and Xerox employees is in APL.

Mattern suggests a data model which includes Transaction Tables — raw operational level data — and Structural Tables — rules for combining and aggregating the raw data. He contends that such a data model can be used to bridge the gap between the available mass of transaction data and the requirement for information to support decision making for planning and control. The model is easily implemented in APL, and can serve as the foundation upon which DSS can be built.

Beyond the data model, Mattern provides some specific guidelines for developing DSS user interfaces. His approach is based on using a set of standard functions and prompts for the data entry and report generation components of the DSS. These are at once easy to use, exploit the commonality of these functions across many systems, and are flexible enough to allow the user to maintain control over the interactions with the system.

THE EVOLUTION FROM MIS TO DSS: EXTENSION OF DATA MANAGEMENT TO MODEL MANAGEMENT

Bonczek, Holsapple and Whinston, like Mattern, are concerned with the pieces from which DSS are built. They suggest that a DSS can be viewed as including 3 subsystems — a Language System, a Knowledge System, and a Problem Processing System (PPS). These 3 systems must enable customization for particular decision contexts. The authors show how generalized data-base management systems and report writers (these are, in essence, the components discussed by Mattern) provide a partial ability to customize systems through generic capabilities to *extract* and *present* existing data values. They point out that what is still required, however, is a generalized ability to *process* data, to apply models to existing data in order to create new data or information. They suggest that a generalized problem processing system (GPPS) can be constructed to provide this capability.

The authors discuss the types of capabilities that will be required in a GPPS, including the types of application specific knowledge which must be available to the GPPS. They show how predicate calculus (in particular Horn clauses) can be used to represent much of the required knowledge.

PROTOTYPING FOR DSS: A CRITICAL APPRAISAL

The paper by Henderson and Ingraham is also concerned with the development of DSS. Unlike the previous 2 papers which focused on the pieces from which these systems are constructed, this paper focuses on the *process* by which DSS are built. Since DSS often venture into new territory (new to the organization, at least), prototyping is frequently suggested as a design strategy. The advantage normally claimed for prototyping is that it explicitly recognizes the need for learning during DSS development, and allows for that learning and the consequent modification of system specifications.

Henderson and Ingraham have tested the prototyping strategy in a case study of DSS development. Though the authors do not describe it as such, their approach to investigating this problem is a good example of action research. Their results show that prototyping leads to rapid convergence on a design, and they suggest that this may result in missing or ignoring important information requirements.

These results raise several important questions about this widely recommended design strategy:

1. Does it lead to inferior DSS designs?
2. Does it lock people into inappropriate decision processes?
3. Does it lose the potential for creativity that is present in other, more group oriented, design processes?
4. Should prototyping be used in conjunction with other design strategies?

The authors discuss these, as well as other, questions.

In addition to the discussion of prototyping, this paper describes a sophisticated model-based DSS designed to support a multi-person decision problem in the public sector. Most readers will find this description both interesting and instructive.

OPTIMIZATION IN INTERACTIVE PLANNING SYSTEMS

The paper by Hurst and Kohner focuses on the role of man-machine interaction in problem solving, especially in the context of planning systems. The authors discuss the concept of Human Aided Optimization (HAO) and present the requirements for an HAO system. They describe a prototype HAO interface which has been developed for a commercially available financial planning system. After outlining the necessary components and capabilities for a computer-based planning system, the paper presents an example of the use of the prototype HAO interface with the financial planning system. The author's message is clear: HAO is a feasible and very flexible technique.

One very useful feature of this paper is an extensive annotated appendix which demonstrates the use of the HAO/financial planning system. The example presented demonstrates how such a system can handle multiple, shifting constraints, and how it can use different optimization (search) methods at different stages in the problem solving (planning) process. The appendix shows clearly how the user is able to control and direct the problem solving process.

DECISION SUPPORT SYSTEMS FOR FLEET PLANNING

Edelstein and Melnyk's paper describes a collection of integrated decision support systems in use at The Hertz Corporation. These systems were designed to support Hertz' major resource allocation problem at 3 levels:

* long range: fleet size planning, additions and deletions,
* short range: daily availability planning, and
* very short range: hourly availability planning and control.

These systems enable Hertz managers to make decisions based on known, recurrent factors — e.g., seasonal demand patterns — and to react quickly to unusual events. Thus, these DSS make all the difference between being able to respond adaptively, to take advantage of unique events — resulting in increased revenues — and not being able to respond quickly — resulting in reduced profitability and the loss of customer good will.

The paper is of interest on a number of levels. It provides a nice example of breaking up a complex problem into slow, medium and fast changing components, thus dealing with the whole, multilevel problem through this set of components. This illustrates one way to structure complex planning problems to make them more amenable to computer-based support, and is a technique which may be appropriate to many similar problems.

The authors show how the systems were sold to Hertz managers as tools for exploring the likely results of tactical and strategic decisions. By turning the computations over to the computer, the DSS leave the managers free to concentrate on devising more effective strategies and tactics for their particular situations. This implementation strategy of demonstrating a clear payoff to the users proved effective in leading to their acceptance and use of the systems.

The paper provides good examples of how fairly simple DSS can be linked with other tools to become much more powerful aids to management. In the Hertz case, the DSS have been linked to sophisticated data-base systems. This assures that managers using the DSS have available the data they require, and also, provides the accumulation of information needed for subsequent analyses. The authors provide several examples of how this facility is used.

The long term system (fleet size planning) provides an immediate, up-to-date description of the current fleet which is used as the starting point in the strategic planning process. This same data base can also be used to explore "what-if" questions about such issues as projected profits or losses from fleet sales.

The data base provides an historical record of rental patterns (e.g., timing, location, rates), which can be used to assess the likely effects of proposed policy changes — e.g., changes in charges for such options as rent here, drop off there.

Even the very short term hourly planning system accumulates data which can be used to optimize the scheduling of support services — e.g., washing, service, maintenance — so that the maximum number of vehicles are available at peak demand times.

DESIGNING A DECISION SUPPORT SYSTEM
FOR A CHANGING BELL SYSTEM

Jeske's paper, like Edelstein and Melnyk's, describes an ongoing DSS application. The system he describes differs from many DSS in one major respect, size. While most DSS are relatively small, often used primarily for ad hoc decision situations, the Bell System DSS is a massive system. It is used at all levels of the decision making process in the largest private organization in the United States (at the time of this writing, at least). In many ways this DSS serves as the "central nervous system" for the Bell System. Its uses range widely, and include selecting new areas for investment and development, assessing the fit of new development with existing lines, etc.

Jeske shows how a large system is built up out of components. He also shows how the planning for such a system must go hand in hand with overall organizational planning. This problem is especially critical in an organization like AT&T which is undergoing massive reorganization. If the DSS should fall "out of synch" with the organization, serious control problems, a sort of "organizational amnesia" could result.

The paper illustrates the problems of controlling the development of large powerful, multi-component DSS. This includes assuring that the parts of the DSS fit together with one another and are appropriately integrated with the rest of the organization's MIS. It also requires that the system be usable by a large number of people in many different parts of the organization. This set of problems is quite different from the more often discussed problems in DSS development and implementation, e.g., tailoring a small system to the needs of a single user. Jeske's paper provides many useful insights into how this new set of problems may be addressed.

APPLYING ARTIFICIAL INTELLIGENCE TO DECISION SUPPORT:
WHERE DO GOOD ALTERNATIVES COME FROM?

The last paper in this volume, by Reitman, provides us with a glimpse of where DSS are heading. Reitman points out that most current DSS help users evaluate and choose among potential courses of action. Unlike a staff assistant (a "human DSS"), however, these DSS cannot *suggest* the alternative courses of action which should be considered. He contends that this deficiency in existing DSS might be met by applying concepts and techniques taken from artificial intelligence (AI).

Reitman describes in some detail an AI system that plays the game of Go. This system is able to work with non-numeric data to develop alternative game strategies, evaluate them, and select the best alternative among them. He provides a detailed description of the strategies employed by the system to find or develop courses of action:

- use of a network of experts at various levels,
- successive refinement of general problems to more specific problems,
- assignment of priorities to situations, and
- use of an "expert and critic" structure.

He shows how the system tests alternatives, and how it limits search in order to keep the problem to a manageable size.

After describing the Go system, Reitman considers how these AI techniques might be transferred to systems in a business context. He identifies problem areas which are likely to prove too difficult (e.g., strategic planning), at least initially, as application areas for AI-based DSS. He also points to some problem areas (e.g., futures trading) which appear to be of roughly the same order of magnitude as existing AI applications, and seem to be promising places to begin exploring the practical use of AI.

CONCLUSION

We began this chapter with some remarks about DSS as a field. Now that we have introduced the individual chapters that follow, we would suggest that the collection as a whole provides a pretty fair sample of the diverse research and practice that characterizes the field. The papers describe some of the many ways business uses DSS right now. They lay out a variety of possibilities for improving current practice. And they invite us to try to understand the structure and promise of the field as a whole. We hope you find reading these papers as profitable as we found hearing them.

DECISION SUPPORT SYSTEMS
M.J. Ginzberg, W. Reitman, E.A. Stohr (editors)
North-Holland Publishing Company
© DSS, 1982

DECISION SUPPORT SYSTEMS: ISSUES AND PERSPECTIVES
by
Michael J. Ginzberg and Edward A. Stohr
New York University
New York, N.Y. 10006

I. INTRODUCTION

The past few years have witnessed the emergence of Decision Support Systems (DSS) as an area of great activity within the information systems field. The pages of MIS and MS journals are filling with articles about DSS. Several conferences on DSS have already taken place and more are scheduled. One major publisher has started a series of books on DSS, which currently includes five volumes. The advertising of DP service providers extols the virtues of their wares as DSS or as components from which DSS can be built. Several academics have been seen criss-crossing the country (and occassionally venturing overseas) trying to win converts to the DSS faith.

What is the basis for all of this action? What is it that DSS does that has not been done before? More fundamentally, what is DSS, and how does it differ from the other computer-based systems organizations have been using for years?

Claims about the benefits and capabilities of DSS are substantial. They will make managers more effective. They will improve managerial decision making, especially in relatively unstructured tasks. They will extend managers' cognitive capabilities, while leaving the manager free to exercise his or her judgement where that is needed. The book is not yet written on what DSS will actually do. Certainly, some DSS have had the types of impacts claimed. Others have not yet shown such a major impact, nor are they ever likely to.

In part, the range of DSS impacts which have been observed stems from the variety of systems which have been labeled DSS. There is at present little consensus about what qualifies a system as a DSS. This paper will begin by examining some of the definitions that have been suggested. It will then examine the implications of these different definitions, focusing on the issues highlighted by *and ignored by* each definition. The paper will then suggest a definition for DSS which highlights those issues we believe are most central to developing and implementing more effective DSS. The remainder of the paper will explore those issues and attempt to outline the areas where further research over the next few years could be most fruitful.

II. DSS DEFINITIONS

The earliest definitions of DSS (e.g., Gorry and Scott Morton[1971]) identify DSS as systems to support managerial decision makers in unstructured or semi-structured decision situations. Two key consepts in this definition are *support* and *unstructured*. First, these systems were meant to be an adjunct to the decision maker, to extend his capabilities but not to replace his judgement. Second, they were aimed at supporting the manager in those decisions where judgement was required, decisions that could not be completely specified as an algorithm and turned over to the computer. Not specifically stated in, but implied by, the early definitions was that the system would be computer-based, would operate on-line, and preferably would have graphics output capabilities.

A refinement of these early definitions is provided by John Little (1970) in his definition of a "decision calculus." He defines this as a "model-based set of procedures for processing data and judgements to assist a manager in his decision making" (p. B470). He argues that in order to be successful, such a system must be (1) simple, (2) robust, (3) easy to control, (4) adaptive, (5) complete on important issues, and (6) easy to communicate with. Implicit in this definition, too is the assumption that the system will be computer-based and that it will serve as an *extension* to the user's problem-solving capabilities.

Throughout most of the 1970's, definitions of DSS like those presented above were accepted by practitioners and researches who wrote about DSS. By the end of the decade, however, new definitions began to emerge. Alter [1980] defines DSS by contrasting them to traditional EDP systems on five dimensions:

1) Use: active (DSS) vs. passive (EDP)

2) User: line, staff and management (DSS) vs. clerk (EDP)

3) Goal: overall effectiveness (DSS) vs. mechanical efficiency (EDP)

4) Time horizon: present and future (DSS) vs. past (EDP)

5) Objective: flexibility (DSS) vs. consistency (EDP)

Three other recent definitions of DSS are offered by Moore and Chang [1980], Bonczek, Holsapple and Whinston [1980], and Keen [1980]. Moore and Chang argue that the "structuredness" concept, so much a part of early DSS definitions, is not meaningful in general; that a problem can be described as structured or unstructured only with respect to a particular decision maker or group of decision makers. Thus, they define DSS as (1) extensible systems, (2) capable of supporting *ad hoc* data analysis and decision modeling, (3) oriented towards future planning, and (4) used at irregular, unplanned intervals.

Bonczek, Holsapple and Whinston [1980] define a DSS as a computer-based system consisting of three interacting components. Those components are (1) a Language System — a mechanism to provide communication between the user and other components of the DSS, (2) a Knowledge System — the repository of *problem domain* knowledge embodied in the DSS, either as data or procedures, and (3) a Problem Processing System — the link between the other two components, containing one or more of the general problem manipulation capabilities required by decision making.

Finally, Keen [1980] applies the term DSS "to situations where a 'final' system can be developed only through an adaptive process of learning and evolution" (p. 15). Thus, he defines DSS as the product of a development process in which the DSS user, the DSS builder, and the DSS itself are all capable of influencing one another and resulting in evolution of the system and the pattern of its use.

These definitions can be contrasted by examining the *types of concepts* each employs to define DSS. This contrast is shown in Exhibit 1. It should be apparent that the basis for defining DSS has been migrating from an explicit statement of *what* a

CONCEPTS UNDERLYING DSS DEFINITIONS

Source	DSS defined in terms of:
Gorry and Morton [1971]	problem type, system function (support)
Little [1970]	system function, interface characteristics
Alter [1980]	usage pattern, system objectives
Moore and Chang [1980]	usage pattern, system capabilities
Bonczek et al. [1980]	system components
Keen [1980]	development process

EXHIBIT 1.

DSS does (i.e., support decision making in unstructured problems) to some ideas about how the DSS's objective can be accomplished (i.e., what components are required? what usage pattern is appropriate? what development process is necessary?)

One result of this migration is a narrowing of the population of systems that each author would identify as DSS — e.g., Keen would exclude any systems which can be built without following an evolutionary strategy, and Moore and Chang would exclude systems which are used at regular, planned intervals to support decisions about current operations. This type of narrowing of a population is indeed a proper function of a definition. By dealing with a smaller population of objects, we can identify those characteristics which the members of the population have in common as well as those characteristics which differentiate one population from another. This helps to focus attention on those problems where research is most needed and is likely to be most fruitful.

Unfortunately, the most recently offered definitions of DSS do not provide a consistent focus, since each tries to narrow the population in a different way. We can consider the types of questions each definition leads us to ask. Following Moore and Chang we would ask, how can you build extensible systems or systems to support analyses which have not been prespecified? Bonczek et al. would lead us to ask how knowledge can be represented in a system and how to provide various problem processing capabilities. Keen's definition would cause us to ask how the development process can be structured to assure that the feedback loops among user, builder, and system are in place and functioning.

While all of these questions are interesting, they collectively ignore the central issue in DSS; that is, support of decision making. There seems to have been a retreat from consideration of outputs, the dependent variable, and a focus on the inputs instead. A very likely reason for this change in emphasis is the difficulty of measuring the outputs of a DSS (i.e., decision quality). While such measurement difficulties no doubt exist, they must not be used as an excuse for ignoring what should be our central concern.

Supporting and improving decision making *is* the issue in DSS. Definitions which attempt to narrow the field, to focus research along some other dimension are missing the point. Indeed, this is the reason why recent DSS definitions have been so inconsistent with one another and have not developed a clear notion of DSS.

We propose that, for now at least, a definition of DSS quite close to the early definitions of Gorry and Scott Morton and Little be adopted. That is, *a DSS is a computer-based information system used to support decision making activities in situations where it is not possible or not desirable to have an automated system perform the entire decision process.* The remainder of this paper will explore some of the implications of this definition: What characteristics are common to all (or most) DSS? What characteristics can differ? What development process (or processes) is appropriate for DSS? What usage pattern (or patterns) is appropriate for DSS? What research is needed to enable us to build better DSS? Perhaps once these questions have been answered it will be possible to draw narrower boundaries around the field, to more clearly define DSS.

III. THE ANATOMY, PHYSIOLOGY AND ONTOGENY OF DSS

The elements that characterize DSS can be separated into three major groups: (1) the underlying technological components from which DSS are built, (2) the ways in which DSS are used, and (3) the processes by which DSS are designed and implemented. These three groups represent the anatomy, physiology, and ontogeny of DSS, and a full understanding of them will provide a relatively complete picture of DSS.

IIIA. ANATOMY: DSS TECHNOLOGY

In earlier work, Keen and Scott Morton [1978] argued that technological issues were secondary considerations in DSS. Advances in hardware and software had made DSS possible, and the important considerations in DSS design involved human decision making. Since that time, research has continued on discovering problem situations where DSS can be applied, on the man-machine interface, on the impact of DSS on individuals and groups, and on the behavioral aspects of implementation. Other research, however, has stressed the hardware and software aspects of DSS, seeking to broaden the domain of application of computer support, to speed the development process, and to make the resulting system more adaptable to the changing needs of decision makers.

In our view, both areas of research are vital to the success of the DSS concept. Technological progress determines what can be done; behavioral research determines what should be done and how best to apply technology to serve organizational goals. Ideally, the latter should drive the former, but it seems that technology has a momentum of its own.

In this section we review DSS technology, the elements which make up a DSS. To be complete, our review should consider both hardware and software. DSS hardware, however, differs little from that for any modern computer-based information system. No special hardware is required for DSS in our view, nor are there any necessary hardware requirements to qualify a system as a DSS. There are some interesting potential impacts of hardware trends for future DSS, and we shall address these in the final section of this paper.

Turning to DSS software, we first consider some suggested taxonomies. The first (Alter [1977]), divides DSS software into seven types based on function performed. Three of the types are *data-oriented*, performing data retrieval and/or data analysis. The remaining four types are *model-oriented*, providing either a simulation capability, optimization or computations that 'suggest an answer'. The IRIS system (Berger and Edelman [1977]) which utilizes a high level interactive query language and data base techniques provides an excellent example of a data-oriented DSS. On the other hand, Hax and Meal's [1977] 'hierarchical' production planning and scheduling system which combines optimization and heuristics provides an example of a model-oriented system. Some DSS, however, (e.g., Holsapple and Whinston, [1976]) seem equally oriented to both data retrieval and modelling while others (GADS, Carlson et al. [1974]) are graphics-oriented. Neither system fits easily in this classification scheme.

Donovan and Madnick [1977], differentiate DSS based on the nature of the decision situation they are designed to support. *Institutional DSS* deal with decisions of a recurring nature. An example is the Portfolio Management System (PMS) which has been used by several large banks to support investment managers (Gerrity, [1977]). Another example is the comprehensive system being developed by AT&T and described by Jeske in this volume. Institutional DSS may be developed and refined over a number of years. *Ad hoc DSS* deal with specific problems that are neither anticipated nor recurring. To support this kind of situation requires general-purpose software for information retrieval, data analysis and modelling that can quickly be customized to a specific application. Donovan [1976] describes the development and use of the Generalized Management Information System (GMIS) to support *ad hoc* decision-making.

A classification scheme with similar implications is proposed by Sprague [1980]. Here the criterion is flexibility and transportability across decision situations. *Specific DSS* are built to support a particular organization and task. An early example is the Potlatch Forests system (Boulden and Buffa, [1970]) which provided an interactive planning system containing a model of the company's operations embedded in FORTRAN code. *DSS generators,* on the other hand, provide more general purpose retrieval and modelling facilities and can be quickly tailored to a specific problem. A survey by Naylor and Schauland [1976] documents a marked growth in the use of DSS generators for the projection of financial statements and the development of more general corporate planning models. Current commercial DSS generators of this type include SIMPLAN (Mayo, [1979]) and IFPS (EXECUCOM, [1979]).

A final classification scheme is based on the *degree of non-procedurality* of the data retrieval and modelling languages provided by the DSS (Bonczek et al., [1980]). Procedural languages require a step-by-step specification of *how* data is to be retrieved or a computation performed. Non-procedural languages require the user to specify only *what* is required. At an intermediate level of procedurality are systems that utilize a command language allowing the user to specify the name of a prespecified report or model. The cartesian product of these three levels of procedurality for data and model-oriented interfaces provides nine different possible classes of DSS. DSS systems have progressed from systems where both data retrieval and modelling is achieved using procedural languages to DSS generators that provide intermediate levels of non-procedurality. An objective of DSS development is to provide easy-to-use non-procedural languages for both the data and modelling interfaces.

The various approaches to classifying DSS are summarized in Exhibit 2. Of these schemes we favor the last. It provides an historical perspective on DSS development and objectives, and focuses on the user interface as a key issue in DSS design.

Are there characteristics of DSS software that distinguish it from other software systems? Not necessarily. We have already argued for a broad definition of DSS which would not exclude a batch-oriented interface. A data base system with a high level query language can be the basis for decision support. Office automation systems with their emphasis on the user interface and possessing such features as high-level languages for defining and processing forms and graphic representations of 'in-baskets', 'out-baskets' and files possess many of the attributes of advanced DSS software.

Nevertheless, distinctive characteristics do emerge when we consider general purpose DSS software and especially software incorporating modelling capabilities. Before discussing these features we note several important objectives. DSS generators exist because they provide a means for satisfying *ad hoc* decision-making support. They speed up the development process for specific DSS applications. To this end they must be adaptable to different decision-making situations and easy to use. Beyond this, the generated systems should possess the same qualities as other good software – accuracy, reliability, maintainability, modifiability and so on.

The major components of DSS software incorporating a modelling capability are depicted in Figure 1, which is based on Sprague and Watson [1976], Bonczek et al. [1980], Haseman and Kellner [1977], and Blin et al. [1978]. A similar architecture was evident as early as 1970 in the Potlatch system cited earlier. The major change in modern design concepts is the attempt to give each component the properties of

DSS SOFTWARE CLASSIFICATION SCHEMES

Source	Classification Scheme
Alter [1977]	Data-oriented vs. model-oriented
Donovan and Madnick [1977]	Ad-hoc vs. institutional
Sprague [1980]	Specific DSS vs. DSS generators
Bonczek, et al. [1980]	Procedural vs. non-procedural

EXHIBIT 2.

independence, generality of function and intelligence. A similar evolution occurred in the development of data retrieval facilities from operating system access methods activated by calls from procedural languages to file management systems and finally to database management systems (DBMS).

The purpose of the *Data Extraction System* is to load the DSS data base with external data and data generated internally to the organization by the MIS system. Although it is generally accepted that a DSS requires less detailed and timely data than operational systems (Keen and Scott Morton, [1978]) this can be a major implementation problem. Since the DBMS used by the DSS may be different from that of the operational MIS and since the data will generally be structured differently, quite complex data conversion operations may be required.

The use of a *DBMS* in a DSS where the major purpose is data retrieval is direct and obvious. One only needs to define the 'schema' for the data base and perhaps provide specially-tailored user interfaces if the data retrieval language associated with the data base is inadequate to the task.

In model-oriented DSS there are several additional functions that might be performed by the DBMS:

1. management of both the inputs and outputs of the models

2. storage and access of the models themselves

3. storage and access of a 'knowledge base' of meta-data concerning the semantics of the models and the structure of their constituent processes.

A major research issue in the application of DBMS within DSS concerns the use of time-series and cross-sectional data in modelling. Existing modelling languages have special facilities for managing such data but are weak in general retrieval capabilities. Conversely DBMS's have powerful retrieval capabilities and can maintain complex data interrelationships; however, special application programming may be required to enable them to handle multiple copies of dynamically generated variable length series data as occurs in forecasting applications. Another DBMS issue concerns the need to store intermediate and final results in the database while the DSS is being used. The structure of this data generally can not be anticipated, giving rise to the need to dynamically restructure the data base schema.

The concept of a *Model Management System* (MMS) is an innovative product of DSS research. Its purpose is to facilitate both the development of models and their subsequent use during sensitivity analyses (Elam et al. [1980]). An example of an operating MMS is contained in Sprague and Watson [1976], and a general discussion is contained in the paper by Bonczek et al. in this volume. There are several unresolved research issues. How can the results of sensitivity analysis be stored in the data base and related to the underlying model assumptions and data values? (Stohr and Tanniru, [1980]). Can decision aids be dynamically constructed from module components thus providing the user with a modelling language with the same level of non-procedurality as advanced data base query languages such as IBM's SEQUEL? The idea is that the user would simply specify the required data items without necessarily being aware that they were not stored in the data base; the DSS would then determine the proper sequence of operations, including models to be applied, and display the desired result. Two approaches involving the use of artificial intelligence techniques are proposed by Elam et al. [1980] and Bonczek et al. [1981]. The first involves the use of semantic inheritance nets (Findler [1979]) for knowledge representation, and the second, the use of the resolution principle of first-order predicate calculus (Nilsson, [1971]). The relative merits of these and other alternatives remain to be investigated.

The *Language Interface Subsystem* consists of the compilers and interpreters that translate the statements and commands used for specifying retrieval requests and defining models. The power of these languages has an important effect on the ease of use of the DSS. Attempts to avoid the complexity of step-by-step procedural specifications have already been mentioned. However, it is not yet clear how much non-procedurality can or should be attained, especially with respect to modelling languages. Another approach in this area is to develop languages that will perform more

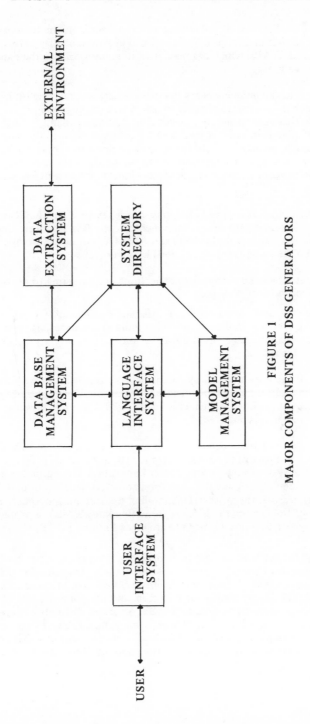

FIGURE 1

MAJOR COMPONENTS OF DSS GENERATORS

computations per character of instruction and avoid some of the tedious details of the control structures and loops of conventional programming languages. A forerunner in this area is APL which has been used in many DSS (see the paper by Mattern in this volume).

Another unresolved issue concerns the use of quasi-natural, English-like languages in DSS. Are such languages truly easier to use? Can they be made precise enough? The answers to these questions are not yet clear (Schneiderman, [1980], Ch. 9). Finally, there is the possibility of including a parser-generator in the language subsystem. This would greatly simplify the process of tailoring the user interface both to the particular problem being addressed and to the needs of the users. An example of a mathematical programming generator system incorporating a parser generator is given in Mills et al., [1977].

The idea of the *User Interface Subsystem* as a separate layer of software lying between the end-user and the other components of the DSS has been used in the DAISY system (Buneman et al., [1977]) and AIPS (Advanced Information Presentation System, Yonke and Greenfield, [1980]). The objectives are:

1. to eliminate the need for special applications programming to generate displays and control the user dialogue;

2. to provide the user with a variety of information channels ('windows') and input-output media including high-level command languages, light-pens and other devices for manipulating visual displays, voice input and output, conventional reports and graphics.

The design of the user interface system provides a fertile area for DSS research. How should the user interaction be managed? When should graphical displays be used? Some guidelines are included in Schneiderman [1980, Ch. 11.]; however, further human factors research is required.

The *System Directory* has been shown as a separate component although it may often be included as part of the DBMS software (Bonczek et al. [1980]). Its function is to give the system some degree of self-knowledge. The purpose is to help the user learn the system, to reduce the need for a complete specification of problems, and to prevent misuse of the system. Outstanding research problems here include the determination of the best methods for representing knowledge — a problem traditionally attacked by artificial intelligence research (see Findler, [1979]).

In summary, the software components of a DSS are quite diverse. No DSS that we know of contains *all* of the components discussed above, though most DSS contain at least some of them. Most of these components can be found in other computer-based systems as well. The Model Management System and the potential role of artificial intelligence, however, seem to be unique to DSS. A further distinctive characteristic of DSS is the attempt to integrate both human and machine decision making into one system. A good example is provided by multiple criteria decision making and other human-aided optimization techniques (see the paper by Hurst and Kohner in this volume).

IIIB. PHYSIOLOGY: DSS USAGE PATTERNS

Many authors have attempted to circumscribe DSS through the definition of "appropriate" DSS usage patterns. This includes who should use a DSS, for what problems, at what intervals, through what mechanism, and to what end. In this section we shall consider each of these questions about DSS use, asking whether any single pattern of use is really more appropriate for DSS than any other.

Much of the DSS literature asserts or at least implies that DSS must be used by managers, or perhaps even upper level managers. But, is such a usage pattern a necessary condition for DSS? We conclude not. While, clearly, many DSS are used by managers, many others exist (or could exist) where this is not the case. Some of the DSS which have been most widely studied and written about are, in fact, used by non-managers at least as much as by managers. The principle users of Gerrity's [1971] Portfolio Management System while often having the title of manager (e.g., Portfolio Manager) are not managers in the traditional sense. Rather, they are investment decision makers, a professional, but not truly managerial role. GADS (Carlson, Grace and Sutton, [1977]), a DSS generator which has been used in a number of real decision situations involving geographic boundaries, has had as users many different "interested parties" to those decisions; but, certainly, they were not all managers. Alter [1980] also describes several DSS whose primary users were non-managerial personnel; e.g., an insurance renewal system used by underwriters.

Note that we are not developing an artificial position by looking at the "hands-on" user of the system and asking whether he (or she) is a manager. Rather, we are considering the position of the consumer of DSS output, the person who directs what analyses the DSS is to perform. In the GADS case, for example, usage is always through a trained intermediary. Our focus, however, is on those people who instruct the intermediary; and, the evidence indicates that these people are quite likely to be non-managers.

What do these DSS users have in common if not managerial status? All are either *decision makers* or key *"stakeholders"* in the outcome of a decision, people who need to understand the implications of decision alternatives and who want to influence the choice among alternatives. Thus, rather than using formal role – i.e., managerial status – as the criterion for defining proper DSS users, it is more sensible to use functional role – i.e., key decision influencers. Perhaps this explains why relatively few top level managers use DSS and why we should not expect them to. Though Mintzberg [1971] describes top managers as the ultimate decision makers for their organizations, in many (if not most) cases this is a misleading description of their role. Top managers are more often *decision ratifiers* than decision makers. That is, their staffs present them with alternatives, recommendations, and rationales to support the recommendations. In many cases, the manager then accepts the staff recommendation and ratifies the *decision* which was *made by* the *staff*. Since it is the staff, not the executive, who goes through the entire decision process, one should expect the staff to be the DSS user as well.

The early DSS literature clearly defines the types of problems for which DSS are appropriate as those which are semi-structured, that is not completely structured at one or more of the problem solving phases – intelligence, design, or choice (Gorry and Morton, [1971]). Further, it is suggested that DSS are most appropriate to strategic planning, rather than control, problems, a theme which has been reiterated recently (Moore and Chang, [1980]). To what extent should the characteristics of problem structure and problem level (planning vs. control) constrain the definition of DSS?

Moore and Chang [1980] argue that problem structuredness cannot be defined in absolute terms, hence they dismiss it as a meaningful concept for defining DSS. While their premise is no doubt true, we cannot accept their conclusion. Degree of problem structure, even if it can only be discussed with reference to particular decision makers, is central to DSS. At one extreme, if a problem can be completely structured to the satisfaction of some decision maker, an algorithm can be written to replace the human decision maker. If no judgement is required – i.e., the complete decision process can be specified – decision support is not an issue. At the other extreme, if no structure can be brought to the problem, that is if none of the data requirements nor any of the necessary processing at any problem solving stage can be specified, decision support is impossible. It is only between these extremes that DSS is relevant, and we agree with Moore and Chang that the location of the extreme points can vary across decision makers.

What does it mean to say that a problem is semi-structured? In essence, it means that it is *possible to bring some structure* to bear on the problem; that a decision maker is willing to accept a certain data set or certain processing routines as relevant to problem solution. Indeed, in a recent paper Alter [1981] points out that a good DSS brings *as much structure as possible* to the problem. While we would change this to as much structure *as the system user will accept,* we are fundamentally in agreement with Alter. Thus, rather than defining DSS as systems appropriate to partially structured problems, they are better defined as systems applicable to problems which are at least partially, but not completely, *structurable.*

Does it matter to what phase of the problem solving process this structure is applied? We conclude not. Structure should be brought to bear on any phase of the process where it is appropriate – i.e., definable and acceptable to the decision maker. Indeed, the DSS described in the literature show examples of support for all phases – intelligence or problem definition, design of alternative solutions, evaluation of and choice among the alternatives, as well as monitoring and control of implementation of the chosen solution. Of course, the type of support will vary from phase to phase since the nature of the activities varies. And, some phases are more easily supportable than others; hence, they are more likely to receive support. In particular, support for the design phase typically requires much more problem domain knowledge embedded in the system than is the case for the other stages. Consequently, relatively few DSS support design. Reitman (in this volume) discusses the application of artificial intelligence techniques to alternative generation, i.e., the design phase.

As stated earlier, many authors view DSS as appropriate only to future oriented, planning problems, not to current control problems. We find this distinction hard to accept. In what way is the decision process for (1) planning next year's operations of a complex manufacturing facility fundamentally different from that for (2) analyzing last month's sub-standard performance of the facility in order to design a corrective course of action? Both require completion of the entire intelligence-design-choice-implementation cycle. Neither is likely to be totally structurable, nor is either likely to be completely unstructurable. In other words, each would appear to be a candidate for a DSS.

One of the more recent trends in delimiting DSS is to state that they are systems whose usage patterns will evolve (e.g., Keen [1980], Moore and Chang [1980], Sprague [1980]). In a sense, this is undoubtedly true. Usage patterns for *all* systems, not just DSS, evolve. Additional data items are placed in an employee master file and the payroll system becomes a personnel system. New reports are added. On-line inquiry and update are added. Evolutionary usage is not unique to DSS.

The argument made by those who claim evolutionary usage as a hallmark of DSS is that use will lead to learning which will lead to new demands on the system, which will lead to refinement of the system, which will lead to new usage patterns, and so forth. There seems to be some confusion here between DSS and novelty. *Any* system — transaction processing, word processing, DSS, or what have you — that represents an initial effort in an area for the user organization is likely to evolve, both in form and in usage pattern. Perhaps *some* DSS will evolve more rapidly than other systems because they start with less structuring and thus have more "room" for change. This will not necessarily be the case for all DSS. In some, the initial structuring may be all that can be accomplished for quite some time; thus, the usage pattern may be relatively stable for a protracted period. In summary, evolutionary usage does not appear to be a particularly useful way to characterize DSS. It fails to distinguish DSS from other computer-based systems, and ascribes to all DSS something which is characteristic only of some.

Several other characteristics of DSS usage patterns are frequently suggested. These are: (1) voluntary usage (e.g., Lucas [1978]), (2) interactive usage (e.g., Scott Morton [1971]), and (3) unplanned usage (e.g., Moore and Chang [1980]). In general, DSS users do have greater discretion about both type and amount of system use than do users of more conventional computer-based systems, e.g., transaction processing systems. Two caveats are necessary, however. First, voluntary usage does not distinguish DSS from other innovative systems, e.g., office automation systems. And second, what appears to be voluntary usage of a DSS may not always be so. In some cases, a DSS is the only available source of information a user needs to do his job. Thus, while use may in theory be voluntary, some amount of use becomes mandatory.

Next to use in support of semi-structured problems, perhaps the most frequently mentioned characteristic of DSS is interactive usage. Initially it was argued that interactive usage was necessary so that the decision maker could carry on an uninterrupted dialogue with the DSS (see e.g., Scott Morton [1971], Carroll [1967]). History has made it apparent that few decision makers want to have on-line dialogues with their DSS. Many DSS are used through an intermediary. In those DSS where the decision maker is the hands-on user, he will, as likely as not, use the system in an "intermittent" mode — executing a few functions, stepping back (perhaps for several hours or even days) to study the result, and then returning to the terminal. Thus, interactiveness is not a good characterization of most DSS. Moreover, technological advance has resulted in many non-DSS (e.g., real-time order entry systems) being converted to an interactive usage mode.

Perhaps more relevant than interactiveness as a characteristic of DSS usage is controllability. This includes availability of the system when the decision maker wants to use it, which often implies an on-line system. But, it goes farther, to what Turner [1980] calls two-way communication. In systems with two-way communication, the user can react to "intermediate" processing results, and direct further processing on the basis of these results. One-way communication, on the other hand, implies that the user can do little to alter the course of processing once it has begun. This two-way communication can take place during a single session at a terminal, over multiple sessions spread out in time, or even with a batch system. This type of controllability is a far more meaningful way to characterize DSS than is interactive usage.

Unplanned usage means different things to different people. To some it means that system outputs cannot be planned in advance. To others it means that usage is aperiodic and cannot be prescheduled. While both are characteristic of many DSS — distinctly more so than they are of conventional systems — neither seems a necessary DSS characteristic. Many decisions recur with substantial regularity in form, in timing, or in both. In the first case, at least some parts of the output can be prespecified; indeed, this is the point of bringing structure to the decision process. In the second case, scheduled, periodic usage of the DSS should be possible. Surely, neither of these circumstances should disqualify a system as DSS.

One final question about DSS usage patterns concerns purpose of use. By far, the bulk of the DSS literature views the purpose of DSS as enhancing an individual decision maker's cognitive capabilities (e.g., Gerrity [1971], Keen and Hackathorn [1979], Stabell [1977]). This view ignores the fact that DSS are used in organizational settings, and do not simply support lone decision makers. Alter [1976] describes the "offensive" use of DSS as tools to bolster an individual's position on a contested issue, to provide the "weight of evidence" to enable him to prevail. Ginzberg [1980] notes that DSS are often used to coordinate decision making activities among the multiple, interdependent participants in a decision. In general, DSS are used to exert control or influence, achieve coordination, as well as enhance cognitive capabilities.

Exhibit 3 summarizes the who, what, how, and why of DSS usage. This summary makes it clear that very few of the distinctions suggested in the literature hold up under close analysis. DSS usage patterns are widely varied. The major commonalities in usage which help define DSS as something unique are that they are (1) largely voluntary, (2) controllable, (3) used by decision influencers, (4) in partially structurable decisions.

IIIC. ONTOGENY: DSS DEVELOPMENT PATTERNS

Much less has been written about DSS development patterns than about usage patterns. Still, some authors have proposed certain development patterns as appropriate to DSS and others as inappropriate. The most common prescriptions for DSS development are that (1) it must include normative decision modelling (e.g., Gerrity [1971], Keen and Scott Morton [1978]), (2) it must be participative (e.g., Schultz and Slevin [1975], Ginzberg [1978]), and (3) it must be evolutionary (e.g., Keen [1980], Moore and Chang [1980], Sprague [1980]). Several other issues about DSS development which should be considered are (1) its focus — on an individual, an organizational role, or a problem, and (2) its orientation towards change.

Normative modelling is the mechanism by which additional structure is brought to unstructured decision situations. That is, the normative model specifies how a decision (or part of a decision) should be made. Thus, if one purpose of DSS is to bring

DSS USAGE PATTERNS

WHO: — Decision influencers

WHAT: — Partially structurable decisions

              — Any/all decision process phases

              — Planning and control

HOW: — Directly or through intermediary

              — Evolutionary, but with widely varying time frames

              — Largely voluntary

              — Controllable, though not necessarily interactive

              — Scheduled and unscheduled

              — Partially prespecified and ad hoc

WHY: — Cognitive enhancement, communication, and control

EXHIBIT 3.

structure to decision making, normative decision modelling is a necessary part of the DSS development process.

The call for user participation in system development is hardly unique to DSS. Indeed, this is one of the most commonly heard prescriptions for developing any type of computer-based system. Since the general case for participation has been amply discussed elsewhere, e.g., Lucas [1978], we will not repeat it here. It should be noted, however, that user involvement in DSS development is perhaps more important than in other, less innovative computer-based systems. DSS often are less well defined, imply greater change, and require more training than many other systems. As a result, user involvement is needed to help resolve design uncertainties and to prepare the users for the new system. It should be noted that while we strongly believe user involvement in DSS development is important, we do not suggest that this should be a criterion for identifying or defining DSS. In some cases, gaining user involvement during DSS development is difficult — e.g., because of a large number of users, or because development is being conducted by an entrepreneur who will later attempt to sell the system. Nonetheless, such systems can be DSS, and Alter [1978] has shown that they are often quite successful.

Recent DSS literature has argued strongly the need for evolutionary design, and Keen [1980] goes as far as saying that an evolutionary design process is a prerequisite for calling a system a DSS. Moore and Chang [1980] state well why evolutionary design is often necessary: the user's problem or problem view changes, hence the system must evolve to remain relevant and useful. However, as stated in the discussion of DSS usage patterns, not all DSS will experience rapid evolution in usage, while some non-DSS will. Further, Henderson and Ingraham (in this volume) raise some serious questions about the efficacy of evolutionary design for DSS. Rather than requiring an evolutionary design process for DSS, it makes more sense to require a flexible process. Where substantial uncertainty exists about user needs or probable system usage patterns, evolutionary design may well be appropriate. If uncertainty is somewhat less, prototyping may be the best approach to design. And, where little uncertainty exists and a fairly stable usage pattern can be projected, a more traditional, structured approach to design is appropriate. The key is to match the design approach to the needs of the situation (see Alter [1981] for additional comments on this issue).

DSS focus refers to the orientation of the system: towards a particular individual, an organizational role or set of roles, or a specific problem or set of problems. As such, it has implications for system content and usage patterns, but its strongest implications are for the development process. A DSS oriented towards a particular individual should be designed with the needs and preferences of that individual in mind. This includes his/her view of which decision(s) should be supported, how they should be supported (i.e., what models and data are appropriate or necessary), and how data should be presented. That is, the potential user's cognitive style and view of his job are key constraints on system design. DSS oriented towards specific roles are designed with much less attention to *individual* user preferences. Rather, they attempt to support an organizational definition of appropriate decision making behavior for people holding certain positions. Problem focussed DSS are also organizationally defined, but the concern here is with how certain problems should be solved, regardless of who is doing the problem solving. The principal implication of these differences in focus is the source of the models and data which are used to design the system. While normative decision modelling is a part of the development process for any DSS, these normative models must be tempered by the needs of the specific setting. The focus of the system determines where we must look to define those needs.

DSS differ from most conventional computer-based systems in their orientation towards change. Conventional systems, for the most part, attempt to avoid change, to maintain the *status quo* in the organization. DSS, on the other hand, are change inducing; they attempt to alter the way people or organizations define and solve problems. As a result, substantial attention must be paid to defining the organizational changes which are required and to assuring that these changes in fact occur. This implies a very different role for the DSS designer from that common to designers of conventional systems. Keen and Scott Morton [1978] illustrate this difference by contrasting two designer behavior patterns — change agent vs. technician. The substantial change requirements also imply a need for more comprehensive training activities than are normally provided in conventional system development efforts (see Ginzberg [1978]).

Exhibit 4 summarizes these attributes of DSS development. Two characteristics, normative modelling and change induction, do differentiate the DSS development process from that for conventional systems. The requirement of user involvement is similar for DSS and other systems. And, while both type and focus of the design process are important aspects of DSS development, both can vary substantially; thus, neither provides a way to uniquely characterize all DSS.

IV. SUMMARY, TRENDS, AND DIRECTIONS FOR RESEARCH

This paper has presented a rather broad definition of DSS, one that does not attempt to limit the range of such systems by requiring that specific components be included nor that specific usage or development patterns be followed. We feel this broad definition is appropriate, since it leads us to focus on the central issue in DSS — the decision process and how that process can be supported.

In this final section we shall review some developing trends in computer technology and examine their likely impacts on DSS. Finally, we shall identify some of the key directions for research that is needed to improve the quality of future DSS.

First, we turn to technological trends. Continued advances in all aspects of hardware, including higher CPU speeds, will help extend the range of structurable decision situations by making more sophisticated heuristics and, in particular, artificial intelligence applications feasible. However, optimal solutions to certain 'difficult' management science problems are likely to remain computationally infeasible. Communications technology — international, national and local networks, distributed data bases, distributed processing, electronic mail, teleconferencing — will increase the oportunities for coordination of geographically dispersed activities and for collaborative decision making. An example of the use of communications capability in a DSS is provided by the Hertz system (see the article by Edelstein and Melnyk in this volume).

The trend towards the automation of office activities brings the man-machine interface closer to general management. The initial emphasis seems to be in providing clerical support using form-driven systems (de Jong, [1980]). This could be followed by systems that support management by providing an 'electronic file cabinet', meeting schedulers, reminders, electronic mail and telephone messages, etc. (Wohl, [1980]). From here it is but a short step to providing the capability for *decision* support as defined in this paper.

Another hardware trend is the development of cheap and powerful microcomputers and their rapid acceptance by both large and small businesses. This greatly increases the availability of systems that can support decision making. An example is the popular VISICALC system, available on both APPLE and TRS-80 microcomputers, which supports spread-sheet accounting and performs functions similar to DSS financial planning generators. Finally, we should note the increasing availability of devices that support the user interfaces — graphics terminals, voice recognition, and voice synthesis.

DSS DEVELOPMENT PATTERNS

— Normative decision modelling

— User involvement (to the extent possible)

— Flexible design process

— Individual, role, or problem focused

— Change inducing

EXHIBIT 4.

In summary, technological advances will increase the effectiveness of DSS. Computational power will be more readily available and will migrate away from the central DP shop towards the locus of decision making, increasing user familiarity with computers and providing more opportunities for the application of DSS.

These hardware advances will become available to DSS developers in the next few years, but by themselves, they will have little impact on the quality of DSS. Two equally important areas are advances in software and in our understanding of decisions and decision making. While the hardware advances will be made largely outside the DSS community, many of the needed gains in software capability and decision process understanding will have to be made by DSS researchers and practitioners.

In the software area, three types of development seem particularly important. The first is Model Management Systems. These systems are in an early stage of development, and substantial progress in this area seems both necessary and likely. The second is the incorporation of artificial intelligence techniques in DSS software. These techniques have a number of potential uses within DSS, including making the user interface "smarter" and more flexible, and providing better support for the intelligence and design phases of problem solving. The final area where software development is needed is in the Data Base Management System, providing facilities for managing highly dynamic data bases.

We conclude this paper very near where we began, by turning again to the decision making process. Our understanding of decisions and decision making remains quite limited. We need better models of specific decision situations and taxonomies which explain in a meaningful way the similarities and differences across decisions. We need measures of decision effectiveness. Ultimately, our progress in developing better DSS will be limited by how well we understand the needs of decision makers.

REFERENCES:

[1]   Alter, S.L., "How Effective Managers Use Information Systems," *Harvard Business Review,* Vol. 54, No. 6 (Nov. – Dec., 1976), pp. 97-104.

[2]   Alter, S.L., "A Taxonomy of Decision Support Systems," *Sloan Management Review,* Vol. 19, No. 1 (Fall 1977), pp. 39-56.

[3]   Alter, S.L., "Development Patterns for Decision Support Systems," *MIS Quarterly,* Vol. 2, No. 3 (September, 1978), pp. 33-42.

[4]   Alter, S.L., *Decision Support Systems: Current Practices and Continuing Challenges,* Reading, Massachusetts: Addison-Wesley, 1980.

[5]   Alter, S.L., "Transforming DSS Jargon into Principles for DSS Success," presented to DSS-81, Atlanta, Georgia, June 8-10, 1981.

[6]   Berger, P. and Edelman, F., "IRIS: A Transaction-Based DSS for Human Resources Management," *Data Base,* Vol. 8, No. 3 (Winter 1977), pp. 22-29.

[7]   Blin, J.M., Stohr, E.A., and Tanniru, M., "A Structure for Computer-Aided Corporate Planning," *Policy Analysis and Information Systems,* Vol. 2, No. 2 (June, 1978), pp. 111-139.

[8]   Bonczek, R.H., Holsapple, C.W., and Whinston, A.B., "The Evolving Roles of Models in Decision Support Systems," *Decision Sciences,* Vol. 11, No. 2 (1980), pp. 339-356.

[9]   Bonzcek, R.H., Holsapple, C.W., and Whinston, A.B., "Representing Modeling Knowledge with First Order Predicate Calculus," *Operations Research,* (forthcoming).

[10] Boulden, J.B. and Buffa, E.S., "Corporate Models: On-Line Teal-Time Systems," *Harvard Business Review,* Vol. 48 (July-August, 1970), pp. 143-154.

[11] Buneman, O.P., Morgan, H.L., and Zisman, M.D., "Display Facilities for DSS Support: The Daisy Approach," *Database,* Vol. 8, No. 1 (Winter 1977), pp. 46-50.

[12] Carlson, E.D., Bennet, J., Giddings, G., and Mantrey, P., "The Design and Evaluation of an Interactive Geo-Data Analysis and Display System," *IFIP Congress 74* (1974), pp. 1057-1061.

[13] Carlson, E.D., Grace, B.F., and Sutton, J.A., "Case Studies of End User Requirements for Interactive Problem-Solving Systems," *MIS Quarterly,* Vol. 1, No. 1 (March, 1977), pp. 51-63.

[14] Carroll, D.C., "Implications of On-Line, Real-Time Systems for Managerial Decision Making," in *Science and Technology Series,* Vol. 12, Tarzana, California: American Astronautical Society, 1967, pp. 345-370.

[15] de Jong, S.P., and Byrd, R.J., "Intelligent Forms Creation in the System for Business Automation (SBA)," IBM Research Report, RC8599, 1980.

[16] Donovan, J.J., "Data Base System Approach to Management Decision Support," *Transactions on Data Base Systems,* Vol. 1, No. 4 (December, 1976), pp. 344-369.

[17] Donovan, J.J., and Madnick, S.E., "Institutional and Ad Hoc Decision Support Systems and Their Effective Use," *Data Base,* Vol. 8, No. 3 (Winter 1977), pp. 79-88.

[18] Elam, J.J., Henderson, J.C., and Miller, L.W., "Model Management Systems: An Approach to Decision Support in Complex Organizations," *Proc. Conference on Information Systems,* Philadelphia (December, 1980). pp. 98-110.

[19] EXECUCOM, *IFIPS Users Manual,* EXECUCOM Systems Corporation, Austin, Texas, 1979.

[20] Findler, N.V., (ed.), *Associative Networks – The Representation and Use of Knowledge in Computers,* New York: Academic Press, 1979.

[21] Gerrity, T.P., Jr., "Design of Man-Machine Decision Systems: An Application to Portfolio Management," *Sloan Management Review,* Vol. 12, No. 2 (Winter 1971), pp. 59-75

[22] Ginzberg, M.J., "Redesign of Managerial Tasks: A Requisite for Successful Decision Support Systems," *MIS Quarterly,* Vol. 2, No. 7 (March 1978), pp. 39-52.

[23] Ginzberg, M.J., "An Organizational Contingencies View of Accounting and Information Systems Implementation," *Accounting, Organizations and Society,* Vol. 5, No. 4 (1980), pp. 369-382.

[24] Gorry, G.A., and Scott Morton, M.S., "A Framework for Management Information Systems," *Sloan Management Review,* Vol. 13, No. 1 (Fall 1971), pp. 55-70.

[25] Haseman, W.D., and Kellner, M.I., "Decision Support Systems: Their Nature and Structures," *Modeling and Simulation,* Vol. 8 (1977).

[26] Hax, A.C., and Meal, H.C., "Hierarchical Integration of Production Planning and Scheduling," in *Studies in the Management Sciences,* Vol. I, M.A. Geisler (ed.), North-Holland, 1975.

[27] Henderson, J.C., and Ingraham, R.S., "Prototyping for DSS: A Critical Appraisal," *Proceedings of the NYU Symposium on Decision Support Systems,* New York, May 21-22, 1981.

[28] Holsapple, C.W., and Whinston, A.B., "A Decision Support System for Area-wide Water Quality Planning," *Socio-Economic Planning Sciences,* Vol. 10, (1976).

[29] Keen, P.G.W., "Adaptive Design for Decision Support Systems," *Data Base,* Vol. 12, Nos. 1 and 2 (Fall 1980).

[30] Keen, P.G.W., and Hackathorn, R.D., "Decision Support Systems and Personal Computing," Working Paper No. 79-01-03, The Wharton School, 1979.

[31] Keen, P.G.W., and Scott Morton, M.S., *Decision Support Systems: An Organizational Perspective,* Reading, Massachusetts: Addison-Wesley, 1978.

[32] Little, J.D.C., "Models and Managers: The Concept of A Decision Calculus," *Management Science,* Vol. 16, No. 8 (April, 1970), pp. B466-B485.

[33] Lucas, H.C., Jr., *Information Systems Concepts for Management,* New York: McGraw-Hill, 1978.

[34] Mayo, R.B., *Corporate Planning and Modeling with SIMPLAN,* Reading, Massachusetts: Addison-Wesley, 1979.

[35] Mills, R.E., Fetter, R.B., and Averill, R.F., "A Computer Language for Mathematical Program Formulation," *Decision Sciences,* Vol. 8 (1977), pp. 427-444.

[36] Mintzberg, H., "Managerial Work: Analysis From Observation," *Management Science,* Vol. 18, No. 2 (October, 1971), pp. B97-B110.

[37] Moore, J.H., and Chang, M.G., "Design of Decision Support Systems," *Data Base,* Vol. 12, Nos. 1 and 2 (Fall 1980), pp. 8-14.

[38] Naylor, T.H., and Schauland, H., "A Survey of Users of Corporate Planning Models," *Management Science,* Vol. 22, No. 9 (1976), pp. 927-937.

[39] Nilsson, N.J., *Problem-Solving Methods in Artificial Intelligence,* New York: McGraw-Hill, 1971.

[40] Schneiderman, B., *Software Psychology: Human Factors in Computer and Information Systems,* Cambridge, Massachusetts: Winthrop, 1980.

[41] Schultz, R.L., and Slevin, D.P., "A Program of Research on Implementation," in R.L. Schultz and D.P. Slevin (eds.), *Implementing Operations Research/ Management Science,* New York: American Elsevier, 1975, pp. 31-52.

[42] Scott Morton, M.S., *Management Decision Systems: Computer-Based Support for Decision Making,* Boston: Division of Research, Graduate School of Business Administration, Harvard University, 1971.

[43] Sprague, R.H., Jr., "Characteristics of Decision Support Systems," *Computing Newsletter for Schools of Business,* Vol. XIII, 1980.

[44] Sprague, R.H., Jr., "A Framework for the Development of Decision Support Systems," *MIS Quarterly,* Vol. 4, No. 4 (December, 1980), pp. 1-26.

[45] Sprague, R.H., Jr., and Watson, H.J., "A Decision Support System for Banks," *OMEGA*, Vol. 4 (1976), pp. 657-671.

[46] Stabell, C.B., "On Defining and Improving Decision Making Effectiveness," Research Paper No. 289, Graduate School of Business, Stanford University, (July, 1977).

[47] Stohr, E.A., and Tanniru, M., "A Data Base for Operations Research Models," *Policy Analysis and Information Systems*, Vol. 4, No. 1 (March, 1980), pp. 105-121.

[48] Turner, J.A., "Computers in Bank Clerical Functions: Implications for Productivity and the Quality of Working Life," unpublished Ph.D. dissertation, Columbia University, 1980.

[49] Wohl, A.D.; "Replacing the Pad and Pencil," *Datamation*, Vol. 26, No. 6 (June, 1980), pp. 169-176.

[50] Yonke, M.D., and Greenfield, N.R., "An Information Presentation System for Decision Makers," *Data Base*, Vol. 12, Nos. 1 and 2 (Fall 1980), pp. 26-32.

DECISION SUPPORT SYSTEMS
M.J. Ginzberg, W. Reitman, E.A. Stohr (editors)
North-Holland Publishing Company
© *DSS, 1982*

THE INTEGRATION OF BUSINESS INFORMATION SYSTEMS
FOR DECISION SUPPORT SYSTEMS IN APL
by
Robin D. Mattern
Product Manager
Financial Reporting Systems
The Computer Company
Richmond, Virginia
May 22, 1981

*I would like to express my extreme gratitude to my wife
for perservering through all that went into the writing of
this paper. I am also very grateful to her and Bob McGhee
for their help on its preliminary drafts.*

1. INTRODUCTION

The purpose of this paper is to explore what goes into the development of good decision support systems (also referred to as DSS). We are assuming that a company is convinced of the value of extending the accounting and reporting functions to support the management decision making process.

How can we develop a good foundation of data collected through the firm's accounting systems? What is the best way to manage the flow of that data up to the senior management level? And what are the cleanest, direct and most responsive techniques for interacting with a computer system charged with performing these functions? We want to keep the economic gains of instituting standard computer hardware and software programs across all systems and the low risk and flexibility of developing custom system modules that can respond to the needs of specific users.

Computers today are well entrenched in accounting for the on-going operation of business firms. Often however, managers have been frustrated in their attempts to gain timely and relevant information. The information is buried in stacks of computer printouts, but requests to analyze and present the data in new formats often take months to implement. Unfortunately in this rapidly changing world, the assumptions that go into selecting key information are out-of-date by the time it is received.

Why can't managers get quick answers to questions that seek to probe the pulse of their business or simulate the results of their decisions? Questions like:

— What are the most critical variables affecting the success of the business that are under a manager's control?

— What's the total cost associated with a project spanning across many departments and its marginal contribution to the profitability of the firm's products or services?

— How long can the firm wait to begin financing a major expansion program, given different confidence levels in expected interest cost to finance it?

— How accurately are managers budgeting their use of resources when their department's activity level may be beyond their direct control?

— Is the equity position of the firm really increasing or decreasing due to the effects of inflation?

Everyone is well aware of the economic value of information. When received on a timely basis, managers can react to new opportunities or head-off potential problems before they materialize. By automating their manual clerical functions, managers hope to gain better control over the information on which they base their decisions. Unfortunately, the large investment in computer equipment and skilled data processing personnel usually exceeds the original manual costs. But even a small percentage increase in profitability of short term operations and long term investments is enough to justify the added costs.

In Section 2 we develop a framework for thinking about and designing interactive business systems. Since it has been used in the development of so many successful decision support systems, the APL language provides the underlying basis for most of the ideas presented here. Building on this foundation, Section 3 gives some specific guidelines for developing a DSS.

2. GENERAL SYSTEM CONCEPTS FOR DEVELOPING A DSS

2.1 WHY APL IS SO SUITED TO BUILDING A DSS

The many years that have gone into building decision support systems using the APL programming language, provides the basis for presenting what works and what doesn't. Much said here naturally applies to systems written in any language. But many implementors and users of DSS systems written in APL are convinced that they were able to arrive at the key success factors faster simply because of APL. The popular explanation for this conviction is the fast development time of APL programs; but is there more to the language that underlies this claim? Is it the characteristics of the language and its implementation as an interactive time sharing system? Or, is it the conceptual synergy between the people who wrote the language, those who program with it, and those who use the resultant APL systems?

One fact is clear: the historical experience of APL programmers has been in developing decision support systems more than any other application. Granted, APL's inefficient use of computer resources has prevented APL systems from being directly integrated into the data collection systems; but today, with the cost of computer processing power and memory dropping every day, it is reasonable to assume that decision support systems can achieve the flexibility of APL, and have direct access to the raw data representing the most detailed operating activities of a firm.

APL enthusiasts are quick to cite examples of the power of APL:

— "It takes ten times as many programming instructions, and therefore programming time, to write a system in other languages than it does in APL."

— "A majority of all internal computer usage by IBM and XEROX employees is in APL."

Although APL is not as widely used as FORTRAN, BASIC, or PL1, the dedication to the language by those who do use it is very strong. The reasons for this dedication lie in the precise definition of the language itself and in the underlying concepts upon which it was created. Ironically to some, APL has been used to build systems that support the needs of progressive managers more than any other application. By reviewing the characteristics, the concepts, and the history of the language, let's see if we can gain an understanding of why APL is so suited to building good decision support systems.

APL, which stands for "A Programming Language," is composed of over 60 primitive functions that perform different operations on arrays of numeric and written textual data. These functions range from:

- simple arithmetic: plus, minus, times, divide, etc.
- data manipulation: reshaping, selecting, sorting, etc.
- complex mathmatics: trigonometry, linear and matrix algebra.

Beginning APLers can learn to use a small sub-set of the languages' functions. Within a few hours they are able to write simple expressions that one might program on one of today's hand-held calculators. That's not much of an advancement, until the realization comes that an APL expression can work on single items of data, or it can work on many items grouped together into arrays. For example, the expression: "UNITS X PRICES" can produce revenue figures for one time period, multiple periods, or multiple products all at the same time. It is also possible to multiply many unit figures times one common price. It all depends on how much data is held by the two data elements: "UNITS" and "PRICES." A remarkable feature of APL is that the data elements can expand and contract from one to many items to accommodate the amount of information available.

Every primitive function in APL is represented as one or two symbols rather than the mnemonics or words of the other languages. Each function is defined within a concise and consistent set of syntactical rules. Since these rules are not dictated by the rules governing the manipulation of bits and bytes within the computer, APL programmers are free to focus on the requirements of the user and not the computer. Because APL was not originally written as a computer language, many believe it is best used as a means of describing and solving information handling problems.

Implemented solely as an interactive computer time sharing system, APL is an interpretive language, which means that each function symbol is translated to the computer's language as each APL expression is being executed. Other languages require that an entire program of expressions be "compiled" or translated first into machine language before executing the translated version during subsequent passes through the computer. The advantage of an interpretive language is that when the computer discovers an error, it stops the translation and execution of the expression, and lets the programmer fix the error so that it can continue. This process of "de-bugging," which is much faster in APL than in other non-interpretive languages, is one of the major reasons for faster development times in APL.

Beyond the characteristics of the implementation, APL's real power lies in the way it directs one's thinking about how to process information. Because APL can perform the same expression on multiple data values without having to write the code for looping through each piece of data, APL system designers can focus on the real essence of programming. They first analyze the data that will flow through a system looking for common ways to process it. Then the data is grouped into arrays representing time series or tables that hold data in rectangular spaces within the computer. Similarly related data is organized into rows and columns that are simple and easy to comprehend. Programs are then developed that will operate on whatever values are held in the arrays. Finally, the system designer defines the exceptions to the type of data the system's programs are designed to handle. The result is a system with as few data elements and system processes as possible. The system takes on the conciseness and consistency that is inherent in APL.

Due to the symbolic nature of the language, APL was originally used for scientific applications, but its capabilities for performing simple operations on tables of numbers without looping made it a good tool for financial applications. With the advent of a file subsystem for storing large amounts of data, and a formatting capability for producing fully decorated numeric reports, companies like Scientific Time Sharing Corporation, and I. P. Sharp and Associates built successful businesses supporting business applications. They offered access to the language for large corporations not wanting to run an APL time sharing system on their own computers.

No doubt using APL on outside service companies was expensive. It was still a viable alternative for managers who had trouble getting relevant information from their data processing departments when they wanted it. The commercial APL time sharing companies became expert at providing responsive systems to quickly produce this information that the managers sought to support their decision making processes. At first APL systems were custom developed from scratch because of APL's fast development time, but eventually generalized software packages were developed that specialized in the decision support systems their customers were requesting. Today the many in-house APL time sharing systems in the United States are opening up a new market for commercial APL software packages.

In summary then, APL gains its power from the conciseness of its language, the forgiving nature of its interpreter, and the thoroughness of its underlying concepts for organizing and processing arrays of data. Figure 1 illustrates the beneficial role that APL and the people who use it can play in the development of interactive systems in general, and decision support systems in particular.

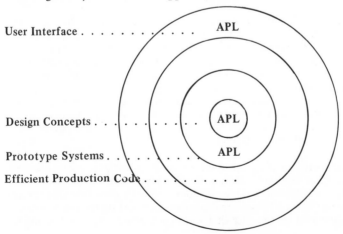

User Interface . . . . APL

Design Concepts . . . . APL

Prototype Systems . . . . APL

Efficient Production Code . . . .

FIGURE 1
THE ROLE OF APL IN THE DEVELOPMENT OF DSS

At the user interface perimeter of the system, APL's time sharing orientation is of great value in developing user-friendly computer dialogue. Limited portions of the language are easily taught to users who need to communicate simple arithmetic and logical expressions to their systems. The data processing concepts inherent in APL make it a great language for people who want to design complex systems. APL's fast development time makes it ideal for the development of prototype systems. When the systems have stabilized, they can be re-written in the other more efficient compiled languages.

2.2 TWO VIEWS OF THE DATA REQUIRED BY DSS

Small decentralized systems give the end users much more control over their application but the consequences of many users doing their own thing can be counter-productive. Large centralized data processing shops do a fairly good job of collecting and storing data, and reproducing it in the format it was entered, but they often are not very responsive in meeting management's need for reporting the data. Their systems generally make the most efficient use of the computer, but the users may be grossly underserved. The question is how do we integrate the two approaches to obtain the best of both worlds.

This integration can only be achieved through communication between individuals who understand the building and maintenance of computer systems, and those who use and understand the requirements of decision support systems. Both groups of individuals speak in terms unfamiliar to the other. Finding people that can relate to both sets of problems is difficult, but by reconciling the interests of both groups during the design phase, where they can reach a consensus on what the system should, could, and will do, good responsive systems can emerge within a reasonable time frame.

Usually the users of business information systems are proponents of the decentralized approach, and established data processing personnel are proponents of the centralized approach. Probably the most important distinction between these two groups of people is the way in which they visualize the information that is processed by their systems. In the next section, we will present a way of looking at the information in terms that are understandable by both groups. From a common understanding, developing the other aspects of interactive business systems should come much easier.

2.3 CONCEPTUAL ORGANIZATION OF A
BUSINESS INFORMATION DATABASE

The management information in most APL decision support systems is manually transferred and transformed from the transaction accounting or budgeting systems. The integration of decision support, budgeting, and accounting data would eliminate this manual transfer and provide us with a unified business information system. In addition to presenting the various types of systems, the pyramid in Figure 2 gives a good representation of the amount of data that is required for three different types of system functions that are appropriate for the different levels of the firm.

LONG RANGE
STRATEGIC PLANNING

ECONOMIC   FINANCIAL
FORECASTING   MODELING

MANAGEMENT   COMPLIANCE
REPORTING   BUDGETING   REPORTING

GENERAL LEDGER

PURCHASING   ORDER ENTRY
ACCOUNTS   OPERATIONS   FIXED   ACCOUNTS
RECEIVABLE   CONTROL   PAYROLL   ASSETS   PAYABLE

FIGURE 2
SYSTEM FUNCTIONS AND LEVELS

The higher the managerial level, the less data is needed; however, it is essential that it has a sound basis in the transaction files of the firm. This data is often much broader in scope and includes information outside the company since high level decisions must be made in relation to the environment in which the firm is doing business.

In the next three sub-sections, we look at the characteristics of business information across all three levels. We will identify three types of tables to hold the information in a clear and simple manner. The transactional data collected by the lowest level accounting systems naturally can be held in transaction tables. We will see how descriptive information that relates to the firm's organizational structure can be held in structural tables. From that basis we will develop a conceptual framework for organizing the information into financial tables that are suitable for management reporting and decision support systems. In the end, we should have a fully integrated user's view of a total business information database.

2.3.1 TRANSACTION TABLES

As stated previously, the firm's accounting systems track the flows of goods and services that are purchased and produced, and the dollar amounts associated with them. In addition to recording the quantity, value, time, and description of each transaction, these systems also identify the organizational structure of the business. At the very least, each record contains an association with a business unit and a general ledger account; it could also hold information to distinguish between actual, budget, or plan data. Double entry bookkeeping systems also must record the offsetting transaction and whether it is a credit (CR) or a debit (DB). Figure 3 (see next page) illustrates what a sequence of 9 transaction records arranged in a tabular form might look like.

These transactions represent the start-up of a new business as they might be entered into a general journal. The business unit codes identify departments for the transactions associated with production and selling, and also those made at the corporate level. If a record contains the same information as the one above it, then the data is not printed. As a means of storing and transferring data between systems, these records could be for purchases from an account payable system, labor and material from an inventory control system, machinery and equipment from a fixed asset tracking system, or invoices from an order entry system.

Depending on the type of records or the nature of the business, other information may be necessary to fully identify the transaction: the currency denomination of the monetary value; the unit of measure of the firm's goods and services; the method of depreciation for each type of fixed asset. Much of this information need not be stored with the original record since the system could look it up in a unit, account, or product listing. For instance, by knowing the date and the country in which a transaction was made the system can easily look up the proper exchange rate in effect at the time of the transaction. This type of information can be held in secondary files that contain more data about the identifying attribute.

Sometimes, however, the information could be different for each transaction. For example, if a special exchange rate is agreed upon the capability must exist to override the standard rate in the supporting table. Usually, though, these supporting files hold information about the data items that need not be repeated with every transaction.

NO.	UNIT	ACCOUNT	DATE	AMOUNT	DB/CR	DESCRIPTION
1	CORP	CASH	1/23	1800	DB	Secure owner's equity
		STOCK			CR	
2	PROD	NFA	4/25	300	DB	Purchase equipment
		CASH		200	CR	Paid for with cash, and
		DEBT		100	CR	A secured note from the bank
3		INV	5/02	900	DB	Inventory raw material
		CASH		400	CR	Paid for with cash, and on
		A/P		500	CR	Credit with supplier
4	SELL	CASH	8/16	800	DB	Credit cash sales, and
		A/R		200	DB	Charge account sales for
		REV		1000	CR	Sale of finished goods
5	PROD	COGS		600	DB	Expense production costs
		INV			CR	
6	SELL	EXP	8/31	120	DB	Expense selling costs
		CASH			CR	
7	CORP	EXP	12/31	30	DB	Deduct depreciation
		DEP			CR	
8		TAX		110	DB	Pay income taxes
		CASH			CR	
9		DIV		40	DB	Pay dividends to owners
		CASH			CR	

FIGURE 3

EXAMPLE OF A TRANSACTION TABLE

We refer to these lists of supporting information as structural tables since they keep information that defines the characteristics of the transaction data as it relates to the overall structure of the firm's data. This differentiates them from transaction tables that keep records of the lowest level data that tracks the basic operations of the firm.

2.3.2 STRUCTURAL TABLES

Structural tables can be simple lists that hold information about the descriptor items in each transaction record. But in order to summarize or consolidate the information, the structural tables will have additional records that represent groupings of the input level identification data. For instance, if the lowest level organizational business units were cost centers, then only cost center identifiers would appear in the transaction tables. The departmental units that represent the sum of a group of cost centers would be described in the structural table. Input information cannot be directly entered to a departmental unit since it is strictly defined as the combination of items subordinate to it.

Thus the structural tables contain input level and summary level items or records that define the reporting structure for the data. These hierarchies can be as simple as summarizations associated with a chart of accounts structure or an organizational consolidation structure. Or the hierarchies can result from the relationships that exist due to a particular summary item being defined as a calculation incorporating other items. In Figure 4, a chart of accounts hierarchy that would be used in a financial planning system rather than in a general accounting system, illustrates both the structure inherent in the accounts and the calculations that might define that hierarchical structure.

NO.	MNEMONIC	ACCOUNT NAME	DEFINITION
1	CASH	Cash and Equivalents	INPUT
2	A/R	Accounts Receivables	INPUT
3	INV	Total Inventories	INPUT
4	GFA	Gross Fixed Assets	INPUT
5	DEP	Accumulated Depreciation	INPUT
6	FA	Net Fixed Assets	GFA − DEP
7	ASSETS	Total Assets	CASH + A/R + INV + FA
8	A/P	Accounts Payable	INPUT
9	DEBT	Long Term Debt	INPUT
10	LIAB	Total Liabilities	A/P + DEBT
11	REV	Total Revenues	INPUT
12	COGS	Cost of Goods Sold	INPUT
13	EXP	Total Expenses	INPUT
14	TAX	Income Taxes	INPUT
15	NIAT	Net Income After Taxes	REV − (EXP + TAX)
16	DIV	Dividends Paid	INPUT
17	EARN	Retained earnings	CUM (BEG EARN) + NIAT − DIV
18	STOCK	Paid in Capital	INPUT

NO.	MNEMONIC	ACCOUNT NAME	DEFINITION
19	EQUITY	Shareholder's Equity	STOCK + EARN
20	LIABEQ	Liabilities and Equity	LIAB + EQUITY

FIGURE 4

EXAMPLE OF A STRUCTURAL TABLE

A transaction table usually has more than one structural table to which it relates data items that describe each transaction. The number of structural tables can be fairly arbitrary. For instance, the account code that is entered in most general ledger systems contains a few digits for the cost center or department, and some for the account. Instead of having one huge table for all unit/account combinations, the total number of structural records would be significantly reduced by breaking the single unit/account code in two and forming two structural tables. For instance, in a company with 20 organizational units and 80 accounts, the total number of items in the two tables would only be 100 (i.e. 20 + 80), instead of 1000 items that would be in the one table if every unit had an average of 50 accounts (i.e. 20 x 50).

However, if there isn't much repetition of items, then one table makes sense. For instance, in a company that is organized so that each department works on only a few of the firm's products, and there are not too many cases where more than one department is working on the same product, then it makes sense to keep the organizational and product hierarchy within the same structural table. If 15 products were being worked on by the 20 departmental units in the above example, there may be only 25 unit/product combinations (i.e. at least 5 units must work on two products). This is still less than the 35 items (i.e. 20 + 15) that would have to be maintained in two structural tables.

So the number of structural tables depends on how the company is structured. As a general case, however, four standard structural tables often make the most logical sense:

UNITS: The organizational business units
ACCOUNTS: The chart of accounts
DATATYPES: The type of data (actuals, budgets, plans, etc.)
PERIODS: The time periods during which the transaction occurred

Figure 5 illustrates the 4 basic dimensions of a firm's financial information. The elements of each are defined by a structural table.

2.3.3 FINANCIAL TABLES

If we take any two structural tables and place the items from one down the rows of a page and the items from the other across the columns of the page, we get a two dimensional table of data; one for each combination at the intersection of a row and column. Every combination may not be valid; as in the first example above, 600 positions in the table would have no information (i.e. 20 possible units times 80 pos-

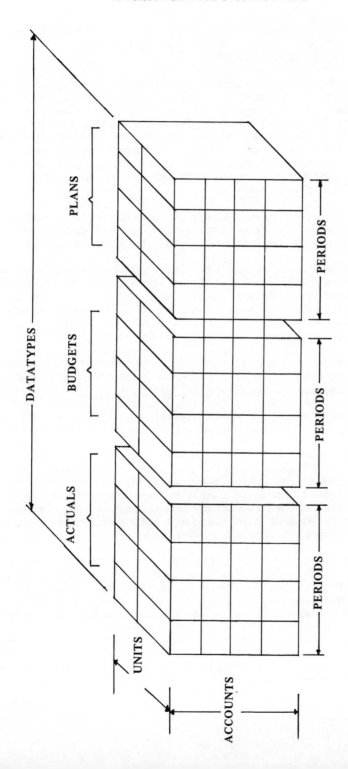

FIGURE 5

DIMENSIONS OF INFORMATION FOR A FIRM

sible accounts less the 1000 actually in existence). But even so, by putting the data into a nice rectangular format, we've created a financial table similar to the numerical spread sheets that we are all familiar with.

Financial tables hold information representing the raw data from the transaction tables, but it is usually in summarized form. The basic summarization occurs during the closing of each accounting period. This process adds up all of the dollar amounts for every unit/account combination and thus gives us one unit by account (or account by unit) financial table. Each subsequent period, another financial table is produced that could have one or more business units across the columns depending on which ones had transactions during each period. Now with more than one period of data, we can also create two other types of financial tables: accounts by periods for each unit, and units by periods for each account.

Using the data from the transaction table illustrated in Section 2.3.1, Figure 6 (see next page) illustrates how this summarization process would occur in four tables, one for each quarter, and a table for the total of all units and all periods.

Most numbers can be traced directly to the transaction table, but some represent a combination of transactions. For instance, the 680 cash figure for the selling department reflects the 800 dollars received for the sale of finished goods, as well as the 120 dollars that went towards paying the sales costs. Only the summary account figures in the total column are shown to keep the example clear, (note: all figures can be either account balances or changes in the account since the firm was just formed).

The summarized data represents a database of information about the operations of the firm for each time period. And while the transaction information will certainly be kept for historical purposes, closing the journal transactions each period significantly reduces the amount of data that has to be stored. But even at a summarized level, the firm's total business information database can get extremely large as the number of periods grow and different types of information are stored besides just actual data.

We've seen how combining the data associated with any two structural tables forms a two dimensional financial table. Two financial tables taken together form one three dimensional database. While it is impossible to visualize, we should be able to extend this thought and take two or more three dimensional databases for each different type of data (i.e. one for actuals, one for budgets, etc.) to form one four dimensional database. We could extend this to form as many dimensions as there are structural tables relating to the transaction tables.

For the sake of simplicity, it's best to stick with the four dimensions shown in Figure 6. These are generally sufficient for categorizing the major ways in which users can visualize the corporate database. This scheme has been found to provide the simplest way of organizing the user's view of the information on which managers would want to base their decisions. It has evolved from the perspective provided from programming in APL with its orientation of organizing data into rectangular multi-dimensional arrays. To summarize: data recorded in the Transaction Tables is aggregated according to the structure and rules recorded in the Structure Tables; the Financial Tables display the results for presentation to the user. This conceptual view of business information systems provides a basis for building a DSS.

NO.	ACCOUNT	QTR. 1 CORP	QTR. 2 PROD	QTR, 3 SELL	QTR, 3 PROD	QTR. 4 PROD	QTR. 4 CORP	ANNUAL TOTAL
1	CASH	1800	(600)	680			(150)	1730
2	A/R			200				200
3	INV		900		(600)			300
4	GFA		300					300
5	DEP					(30)		(30)
6	NFA							270
7	ASSETS							2500
8	A/P		500					500
9	DEBT		100					100
0	LIAB							600
1	REV			1000				1000
2	COGS				(600)			(600)
3	EXP			(120)		(30)		(150)
4	TAX						(110)	(110)
5	NIAT							140
6	DIV						(40)	(40)
7	EARN							100
8	STOCK	1800						1800
9	EQUITY							1900
0	LIABEQ							2500

FIGURE 6
EXAMPLE OF A FINANCIAL TABLE

2.4 INTEGRATING THE BENEFITS OF STANDARDIZATION
AND CUSTOMIZATION

The common element in the previous discussion is that a conceptual integration of the firm's total business information system provides a significant step towards giving managers easy access to company information by using terms they understand. A quite different view of the data is held by data processing people who are charged with organizing and processing the data that tracks the company's operations. Instead of being concerned with the quality and content of the information, they look at the quantitative characteristics of the data — what terminals are best suited to collect and report the data, how it is transformed by computer processors, and what is the best storage device for it. The majority of the tasks that computers perform for businesses are basically filing and typing operations, and data is seen as almost devoid of meaning.

The organization and storage of a business information database can follow any of the following schemes.

- The user's conceptual view
- The availability of storage space
- The frequency of use of the data
- The sequence in which the data is entered

From an efficiency point of view, storing data according to a conceptual organization is usually a poor choice. A trade-off is necessary because response time is such a key factor in the success of a DSS. But users of financial systems must also have the flexibility to change the structure of the data as they perceive the changes; just as APL allows users to put data into arrays that can expand and contract according to the number of data items that are required. APL techniques can be used to integrate data between systems that could exist in separate computers in different locations. The conceptual view of the data is independent of how the data is physically stored.

The design of a good system should standardize as much as possible without sacrificing flexibility. Standard guidelines can be followed at any of four levels of a system:

- The conceptual design and/or data orientation
- General system processes throughout the system
- Specific user activities
- Detailed custom implementation for each user

Standards are rules that have a universal application most of the time. Even at the lowest level, custom solutions can be implemented according to general characteristics about the system process being customized. Coming up with the proper balance between standard and custom procedures or values isn't that hard to achieve if the system is built according to a modular design. Each module represents an aspect of the system that might be changed. If there is only one version of the module, then it represents a system wide standard. Where many versions exist, the system will become highly flexible. Figure 7 illustrates the relationships between the various modules and the required and resultant data for each of those modules in a hypothetical system.

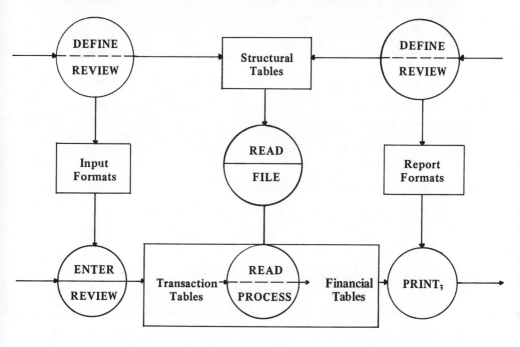

FIGURE 7

MODULAR STRUCTURE

Each of the boxes represents tables of data, and the circles between them represent the program modules that take the input data from one side and produce the output data on the other. As the users of the system enter different tables of input data, different versions of the data move through the system. Each of the data tables, whether they be user input or the result of an intermediate process, can hold many versions of data for the system to process using the same consistent programs over and over.

In more flexible systems, not only are there many versions of the data, but there are also many versions of the system processes and system parameters. If the mechanisms are built into the system to manage all these different versions, users can request that an existing module be modified, or completely re-written to suit their need. For the most part each user will end up with one set of modules that looks like a traditional system. A user profile would be set up that identifies local copies of each system module for each user. Those users who want to be able to pick and choose between different modules will be asked to identify one unique set of system processes each time they use the system. Unfortunately, the price for added flexibility is that more decisions have to be made in order to select from the expanded number of options available.

In summary, a modular structure allows a system to achieve a high degree of standardization and can accommodate whatever amount of flexibility and customization the user will ultimately need. It may not seem necessary at first, and it will most certainly add to the processing costs of the system, but the costs associated with adapting the system to the changing needs over the long run will be much less.

One final but important point — no system will be successful without good readable documentation! Ideally the system specifications, written prior to system development, will provide the basis for the three kinds of documentation: the system maintenance manual, the user's operating manual, and an instruction guide. The first two can be written in technical terms, but the third must be written in terms that explain the purpose and use of the system in the user's language.

3. GUIDELINES FOR DEVELOPING A DSS

On the surface all computer applications perform the same basic functions:

— Definition of data elements and system parameters
— Input of data element values
— Execution of system processes and
— Output of data element values

The last three functions are always required; the first may or may not be required depending on whether the data structure organization is left under the control of the end user or perhaps a system steward. While this makes for a much more flexible system, often the system can be written more efficiently when a fixed data structure is assumed.

Since the execution of system processes can almost always be automatically called into action by the system, we will focus on only the input and output portions of the system. Generally these functions are the user activities that represent the most customized, tailored portions of any system. In order to distinguish between the varying degrees of standardization throughout a system, we will look at them from the perspective of:

— The characteristics of the users' activities
— The general system processes that pertain to all activities

We will present standard features as they relate to interactive decision support systems as well as the total business information system. We may be able to cover as much as 80% of any typical system, but we will also note the nature of custom features that would exist in a flexible system.

3.1 USER ACTIVITIES

Once the structure of the firm's information has been understood and defined, the focus of our attention should turn to the users who will be using the decision support systems or the underlying business information system. When a user sits down to use a system, (s)he really has only two concerns: input and output. The intermediate logic that produces the results from the input data is important, but the user should not have to take an active step to invoke execution of it.

To clarify these two basic user activities, we defer until the next section those aspects that are common to both, such as selecting the data elements to be input or reported. In this section we discuss only a general framework for each of these two user activities because they are usually the most customized aspects of a system. Afterall, it's the interface to the most specific needs and concerns of the people who use the system that ultimately determines the success or failure of that system.

3.1.1 INPUT PROCESSES

In this section guidelines are presented concerning the three basic types of data that the user of a business information system would be entering or making changes to:

1. Structural data that defines the user's view of the firm
2. Transaction data that tracks the firm's operating information
3. Financial data that is entered directly into the business information database

Maintenance of Data Elements

If a system has been designed to accommodate flexible data structures, a user or a more sophisticated system steward will have to define the data elements for those structures. The steward is responsible for the initialization of the system's data elements, and for making changes to them on a periodic basis. This is accomplished through the following four activities:

1. Enter/change data element attributes. Every data element is given a name, description, reference identification, and other information that characterizes the data item values it will represent. This is a simple process similar to raw data entry.

2. Define data element structure. The relationships of the data elements to other data elements are specified to form a data element structure. Possible techniques for doing this are as simple as making a direct link to another data element or as complex as defining logical or arithmetical relationships.

3. Delete data elements. The system can be instructed to ignore data elements that don't have any value for particular time periods. These data elements can be flagged as "pending deletions," and actually deleted by the system steward since this process is expensive, and can have many complex ramifications. Transactional systems that maintain good audit trails usually don't allow deletions. In systems designed for higher level management, however, data ele-

ments may be deleted when more storage space is needed or when they have out-
lived their usefulness.

4. Move data elements. Changes to the relationships that define the data element
structure can be tricky. The time spent to come up with a good method may
make the simpler method of deleting a data element from here, and re-entering
it there more desirable.

Collection of Transaction Data

There are three basic forms for entering and changing the data that flows through
a system:

— Batch entry through punch card or magnetic tapes
— Line by line entry through a typewriter based terminal
— Screen entry through cathode ray tube terminals

Input formats will usually be custom built for each company, application, input
device, or perhaps even each user. It is good practice to provide these in a generalized
form, that can be used by first time users. When they become accustomed to the input process, they will be in a much better position to specify exactly how to make
the data entry faster by tailoring the input format to the way the data exists in its
physical form.

Adding new records to a transaction table for the first time generally requires the
user to enter data values for a complete set of data element fields that would make
up one complete data record. A good input program has as many features for expedit-
ing this process as possible. Duplication keys allow the user to replicate the values
from previous data entries without having to re-enter them for each record. Default
values for fields that the user may not have a data value for allows him(er) to enter a
complete record and go back to fill in the missing data elements fields later.

The layout of the prompts for entering data into a transaction table often is merely a by-product of the way in which the program code was written. Care should be
taken to place the prompts on the page or screen in a form that parallels the format
so that the input data will be reviewed back to the user for input verification. First
time data entry and subsequent data changes can both follow the same format of reviewing the existing data if previously entered and then changing it. A typical format
might be:

       data elements ARE NOW: data item, data item, ...
              THEY NOW ARE: . . . .

If no previous entries have been made for the data elements, the format for entering new data might be:

       data elements NOW ARE: . . . .

Although a data entry terminal session can leave a messy trail of spaces, improper
entries, and corrections, the spacing of the system prompts, the input position, and
the user's entries on the page, as well as the prompt's grammar and punctuation, can

make the difference between an easy and difficult to use input routine.

Data entry into financial tables is very similar to changing data in a transaction table, but the user will always be entering numbers instead of mixed numeric and character input. Since the structure of the data elements that define a financial table would be changed in another system process, a user performing input will always identify which data element(s) along the rows and columns (s)he wants to change. If it's the first time that the user entered a number for that data cell, the system will, in reality, be performing a data change from zero to the specified amount.

To speed up the data entry process, the system can allow the user to enter calculation codes that generate a sequence of numbers often representing a time series. A list of such codes and a brief description follows:

REPT: Repeat a value for all input periods.
GROW: Inflate a number by a specified compounded percent each year.
PROJ: Project a linear trend based on the available historical data.
PRO2:   Project a second order trend based on the available historical data.
REGS: Perform a linear regression based on the relationship between the values.
SPRD: Spread an annual total across each month of the year.

These codes generally represent relatively simple expressions in APL, but codes are sometimes preferred for the sake of readability. If the user wants to add other calculation routines (s)he can either enter an APL expression directly or have an APL programmer quickly write one and place it into the user's custom input routine.

After the data entry is finished, the user should be asked if (s)he wants to save the new inputed data in a particular alternative version of the financial table before having it stored into the financial database. In order to later identify the table version with ease, a date and time stamp should be associated with the data, an easily referenced mnemonic, and a brief description that explains the reason for the data change. Obviously the user must be given the capability to perform general data management functions of deleting, copying and creating new versions of these tables. This ability to develop many versions of one particular financial table provides a powerful tool for analyzing different assumptions.

Ad-hoc Data Entry

The ad-hoc data entry process is very similar to that for data entry into financial tables. The user selects a table and data element, changes its values, and stores it as a new version in the financial database. But as with changing data in transaction tables, users need the ability to make sweeping changes across a number of tables. Top level managers can use this ability to enforce directives down through the corporate structure. For instance, if (s)he wants to reduce all proposed expense budgets by 10%, this should be done by entering a single expression rather than asking each user at every level to re-enter every expense budget. Careful management of the different versions that result from these kinds of changes has to be considered in order to preserve one copy of the data before it is changed.

One word should be said about controlling who has the authority to make changes to the data and when. System stewards should be able to control the availability of certain input financial tables for data entry between specified periods of time for authorized users. A different set of users would have the authority to review the data or to see its impact on other financial reports.

3.1.2 OUTPUT DATA REPORTING

Most report formats are specific to the company, the application, the manager or the user requesting reports. There are three basic types of reports:

1. Record listings that review the input data in the transaction and structural tables.

2. Financial statements that display input and calculated data from the financial database.

3. Ad-hoc reports that present information on an as needed basis.

General characteristics are associated with these three basic types of business information reports, but first let's review some basic report generation processes that go into any report: selecting, transforming, formatting, decorating, and printing the data:

SELECT: First the user has to select the data that (s)he wants to see on the report. The system's first task is to go get the data from its storage location and produce some sort of rectangular array that represents a sub-set of the transaction files or financial database. The data at this point is either raw input data or calculated data that is up to date.

TRANSFORM: Particularly in the case of higher level DSS, the person requesting the report may want to perform additional calculations on the selected data. These calculations could be simple variances or ratios, or sophisticated analyses of risk. They are only performed for the purposes of a particular report and would not be stored unless the results are deemed noteworthy enough to be stored for further use.

Another type of transformation is to transpose the sequence of dimensions as they appear in the database (e.g., Units, Lines, Data Types, Periods) to appear differently on a report (e.g., Units, Lines, Periods, Data Types). Again this transformation would occur on the selected data array only for the purposes of appearing on a report.

FORMAT: With the numeric data transformed into two dimensional tables, it is now ready for printing. The definition of a report format provides the general framework for a skeleton upon which different data values will be displayed. Neither the data nor the row and column names are known until the report definition comes in contact with the data. The basic layout of the report, with regard to spacing and positioning of the data is part of a static report definition that can be used over and over. With some of the more advanced word processing systems, typists can enter the report layouts onto a CRT screen, just as they would type an actual report complete with descriptive material.

DECORATE: While most of the format for a report can be defined independently of the particular data values that will appear in it, a report can take on different characteristics that depend on the particular values being printed. Examples of this are the flagging of particular numbers on a report with a special character to denote an exception condition, or the replacing of a long name with a shorter name if it was truncated by the cruder parameters for the generalized report definition. Special programs can fine tune the report formats to match the special needs of the people who use the reports. These programs fall into the domain of the programmer rather than the user. They can be tricky to write because they must handle all the possible data arrays that may use the report definition, but once defined they don't change much.

PRINT: Finally we are ready to print the formatted report. But a final set of options need be specified that are subject to being changed with each printing of the report. The most important one is on what type of output printing device the report will be printed. These "print-time" parameters can be associated with practically all types of reports. The system should allow the user to select pre-defined report parameters independently from the data being printed and its format.

The specification of each step could be done each time the user wants to print a report, or they can be pre-defined, stored and used in varying combinations with each other. A set of selected report definitions or parameters for each step would make up a stable production type report. Specifying each at print-time would make for a very flexible report, but also is very time consuming to produce. Obviously the proper balance depends on the nature of the report and who its users are. Thinking of a report in terms of these five basic steps can give users maximum turn-around time and flexibility.

Transaction Record Listings

Record listings are used to display the information in transaction and structure tables. Both transaction tables, in which input data is collected, and the structural tables, in which data element definitions are held, have records containing various data element fields of information. One structural table may only have a couple of hundred records, denoting a product structure for example. Transaction tables have the potential for holding millions of record entries.

These types of files have been the bread and butter of computer systems for many years, so all the possible ways to print them are well understood. Basically these reports are a continuous list of records down many pages with selected data element fields printed across the page. If all the data element fields don't fit across one page, then the entire set of records will be printed on another set of pages until all the desired fields have been printed. To help organize this continuous sequence of records, there are three basic capabilities that are required:

1. Sorting data values within one or more data element fields taken in order of importance (i.e. major to minor order)

2. Producing a blank line or another page at breaks which identify different groupings of the similar data values within one or more data element fields

3. Sub-totaling one or more numeric data element fields at the end of each grouping of records.

While the insertion of breaks and sub-totals may not be required in the structural tables, a particular type of presentation is useful for displaying the hierarchical organization of the data elements. The sequence of records is important, and the use of indentations provides a good visual illustration of which record is dependent on which other records.

Standard Financial Statements

The financial table data from the multi-dimensional financial database is the hardest to get to print onto the two dimentions of a page, or three dimensions if you consider multiple pages. Starting with the four dimensions in the financial database, data elements from the first dimension (e.g. business units) would be placed on each page. Data elements from the second dimension (e.g. line items) would be placed down the rows of a page. The two remaining dimensions of the database (e.g. tables and periods) are placed on the third dimension of the report across the column. The system must therefore collapse the last two dimensions into one. This is easily accomplished as can be seen from the following example:

QUARTER ONE			QUARTER TWO			
		QUARTERLY			QUARTERLY	YTD
ACTUAL	BUDGET	VARIANCE	ACTUAL	BUDGET	VARIANCE	VARIANCE

The third and fourth dimensions have been interchanged or transposed. Note that a different number of data elements from the third dimension were printed with the first two data elements of the fourth dimension. By a similar process of collapsing data dimensions, or nesting the data elements of one dimension within those of another, two or three dimensions can be printed across the pages and columns or down the rows of a two dimensional report. If the collapsing occurred across pages of a report, then there would be one page for each combination.

Once we have one two dimensional array of financial information to be printed on a two dimensional page of a report, the data must be placed within a report format. If we look for common characteristics among all financial statements, we see that they all have the following basic components:

HEADINGS: At the top of the page there will generally be some text that identifies the type of report, one or more data element groups, the date and time the report was printed, and the scale factor or type of units represented by the numeric data in the body of the report.

COLUMN HEADINGS: The data element names from one or more dimensions of the financial database, can be printed as shown in the above example. While names may be longer than the width of a column, the system can automatically stack each word in the name above each other, truncating the longer words. The result is generally acceptable enough, but if it isn't, a special custom decoration routine could always deal with the names that had words which are too long for the column width.

DATA: The data from a rectangular array is printed underneath the column headings. There are many special ways to print numbers. Negative numbers are parenthesized, or all numbers have commas separating every three digits. These formats can be associated with every number on the report in each column or across a line.

MISCELLANEOUS DETAILS: Titles, describing the next group of data, spaces or blank lines, and single or double underlines are placed throughout the data portion of the report. Generally these can be associated with a particular data element. For instance, NET INCOME AFTER TAX could have a double underline above it and below it followed by a space. There are a number of possibilities that may be chosen, but once defined it remains pretty stable. And of course it could always be changed by a special decoration routine for a particular report.

FOOTNOTES: Any type of descriptive material can appear in a designated place on the page, and should thus be provided for even if it it not always used.

Given the basic elements of a report, we can determine the amount of data one might expect to get on a page as the following sequence of rows on a report shows:

data element TITLE

    data element NAME
    data element NAME
    data element NAME
    data element NAME
    data element NAME
    data element NAME

SUB-TOTAL

GRAND TOTAL

There are generally twice as many data lines on a report as there are miscellaneous details. Assuming a minimum and maximum number of the other report elements, you can figure that the average number of data lines on a report is 17 as the following table shows:

	MIN	AVG	MAX
HEADINGS	3	6	9
COLUMN HEADINGS	3	5	7
DATA	40	34	28
MISCELLANEOUS DETAILS	20	17	14
FOOTNOTES	0	4	8
TOTAL	66	66	66

When working with the number of characters that will fit across the page we can assume that we are working with pages that are either 80 or 132 characters across. If a data element name takes up 32 character positions, then there is room for 6 or 12 columns, each with a width of 8 characters, which would fit across 8½ or 14 inch pages. Thus on an 8½ by 11 inch page we can reasonably expect to display 170 numbers: a reasonable amount to be assimilated in one reading.

Traditional computer printouts try to put as much data into every character position of an 11 by 14 inch computer page. That much information can quickly become overwhelming for the manager who wants to select the relevant information at a glance. By manipulating the basic elements of a report, a flexible report writer can significantly affect the designing of good reports.

Ad-hoc Reports

The last type of report is difficult to generalize about because its users are really more interested in focusing on a few selected values and don't really care about the format. With a heavy use of the selection and transformation steps, the information is presented and then usually discarded. All the aspects of a financial report could apply to this type of report, but the amount of information presented would be far less.

While we won't go into detail here, there are many types of plots from very simple line graphs to more sophisticated bar and pie charts that can generally be displayed easily and conveniently with today's plotting devices. When looking at trends and relationships between data element values, there is nothing better than a graph to provide a feeling for the information.

3.2 GENERAL SYSTEM PROCESSES

Finally, there are those aspects of the system that are present throughout all the user activities in any interactive computer application. By focusing on the interaction between the user and the system, we want to give the user control over the system. The more consistent the human/machine interface, the easier it will be to use the system on a daily basis. The following sections discuss four important features that allow users to get what they expect out of the systems they use.

3.2.1 USER CONTROL OF SYSTEM PROCESSES

When a user sits down to use a system, both the user and the system have to have a means of communicating with each other in a way that is understandable by the other. By providing a means of instructing the user in a simple but not demeaning manner, a more enjoyable interaction can be obtained. Here are three ways that the user might control the system activities:

1. Without any prompting from the system, the user enters a mnemonic or sequence of action words expressed together according to a strict set of rules. The instruction is short and concise, but the user must remember what all the possible activities might be. Help is provided as the user can request or look up the list of possible activities either from the system or the documentation. Experienced users like this method to save time, but beginning users find that it requires too much advance knowledge of the system.

2. The system prints a menu of possible choices with a brief indication of what they are. The user then indicates his(er) selection. This can be time consuming as the terminal prints out each menu, but for choosing from among 10 or less possibilities, it is a good technique.

3. The user, through a series of steps, searches through a long list of items using various techniques. The user should be notified to what extend the search has been narrowed down, and allowed to quickly review what (s)he's found so far. The techniques vary according to the particular data organization used, but as mentioned earlier, the scheme should conform to the user's view and not necessarily the computer's.

3.2.2 LOCATION OF DATA ELEMENTS

Once the user has selected the activity that (s)he would like to perform, whether that activity is defining data elements, entering input data or reporting output data, the next step is to locate the particular area of the financial database that is to be changed, added to, or reported from. The user must direct the system to access this particular area, either by explicitly referencing the appropriate data elements, or by indirectly referencing those data elements that have characteristics requiring user attention. The ease with which the reference is made depends on the ways the system is set up to identify data elements. Here are some possibilities:

IDENTIFICATION CODE: This is a unique alpha-numeric code that is automatically assigned to the item being recorded, be it a data transaction or a structural data element such as a financial account or a product component. The system may work well with these codes, but they are very hard for users to remember and are best used only for internal system purposes.

MNEMONIC: A mnemonic is like an identification number, but it is usually assigned by the user and has some meaning to the users of the system. However, when we have to distinguish between several hundred data items, remembering their mnemonic identifiers is as hard as remembering the ID codes.

SHORT and LONG NAMES: Longer in length than the mnemonics, these names can
be used to clearly identify the data item in readable and easy to remember English. They are used primarily during data input or on
page headings, columns, or rows of a report. Due to their length,
and the fact that they are generally not checked for uniqueness,
they are not very useful when trying to select a data item.

DESCRIPTION: Often neglected, it is good practice to have a full description associated with each data element. When there is ambiguity in the
other forms of identification, the user can read the description to
determine the intent of the user who originally defined the data
element.

To locate a data element, the user must enter an exact reference. If the user doesn't
know this, then (s)he has to search the financial database for it — in essence, play a
game of twenty questions. The answer to each question reduces the number of possible data elements until the right ones are found. The menu technique described in
the previous section can be used to locate data elements organized in a hierarchical
structure. For instance, if a user is looking for a particular account, the system might
ask if it's an income, expense, asset, liability, or equity account. If it's an expense account then the system displays 10 or so expense account groupings. The user selects
one group and then selects the right account from those accounts within it. The distribution and structure of the data must be analyzed to come up with the best method.

To indirectly select data elements from a list of many data elements, a more
powerful search method must be used. Generally the search is on data values associated with the data elements that are being searched for and not the attributes of
the data elements themselves. For instance, an executive who wants to reorganize his
sales force along geographical rather than product lines, may search the employee
file for addresses in order to come up with a set of possible branch office locations.
This type of search on transaction files is hard to specify, but the development of
natural search languages, with data management systems, is making them more common in DSS and other business information systems.

3.2.3 PROMPTING CONVENTIONS

A key aspect in making users feel that they are in control of the system is to ensure that the system prompts and responses are clear and consistent. We have already
discussed the types of response for the prompts used during two of the three main
areas of interaction between the user and the system:

- Selecting user activities
- Selecting data elements
- Entering input data

In this section, we will identify a small set of basic types of prompts. We use
standard types of prompts to reduce the ambiguity that often exists as users sit and
ponder what the system expects them to enter in response to a particular prompt.
Here is a description of what the user should enter in response to each type of system request for input:

YES/NO: The users only response is "YES" or "NO" (sometimes just a "Y" or "N" is allowed). While many sophisticated users of computer systems prefer otherwise, these questions are asked in order to get confirmation from the user that a drastic action should indeed be taken, such as erasing a file.

CHARACTERS: The user can enter any valid alphabetic or numeric character. The only restriction may be the number of characters input by the user.

NUMBERS: The user enters a number or a string of numbers. Depending on why they are being requested, they can be whole numbers or can have a decimal portion; they can be selected from a valid list of numbers, or between a range of two numbers. The user may also be required to enter one number only, a specific number of numbers, or up to some maximum number of numbers.

DATES: A special form of input that requires the user to enter a valid date. Checking for the valid days in each month, is not the easiest thing to do if you try to allow for all possible ways people represent dates. Of course it's been done in thousands of systems.

ACTION WORDS: The user enters a word that matches one or more words from a valid list. A nice convention is to allow the user to enter only enough beginning letters of the word to distinguish it from the others in the list.

MIXED INPUT: The user enters data values for a number of different data element fields. The user must enter the data values separated by a delimeter that could never be part of a numeric or character data value. For terminals that can set tab positions at arbitrary positions across the page or screen, the best delimeter is the tab key. This has the effect of lining up all of the user's input underneath the appropriate field name.

EXPRESSIONS: The user enters an expression that either defines how the system should search for a set of data element values or perform a calculation. The user must learn strict rules to be able to enter correct expressions. The efforts to develop natural languages addresses the issue of coming up with a set of rules that are as flexible as English and yet still strict enough for the system to translate it.

It goes without saying that each response entered by the user must be followed by an indication that the user has ended his response and that it's now the computer's turn to evaluate it. On almost all interactive systems, this is indicated by hitting the carriage return.

Two other features that can greatly enhance the user-system interface are:

KEYWORDS: The user can, in response to any system prompt enter words like "HELP," "END," "QUIT," "GO TO____," "GO ON," and "SAME" which have the same meaning throughout the system in a consistent manner. This goes a long way towards reducing the feeling that the system has trapped them at a particular point and they have no recourse but to pull the plug on the machine. The system has to make sure that the data entered so far has been saved in the system's files if a user aborts a particular activity.

BUFFERED INPUT: When users know what the next prompt sequence of system prompts will be and their appropriate responses, they can enter those responses separated by the delimeter. This can greatly facilitate interaction with the system. If a response is incorrect the system must disregard all the remaining responses in the input buffer and prompt for a correct response.

Good systems will have these basic types of prompts, and the appropriate data checks that go with each, written into program modules that can be used over and over throughout the system. The only difference will be the actual wording of the prompts. Not only does this ensure a consistency throughout the system, but it allows programmers to modify these routines should a new input device be needed by the system.

DECISION SUPPORT SYSTEMS
M.J. Ginzberg, W. Reitman, E.A. Stohr (editors)
North-Holland Publishing Company
© *DSS, 1982*

THE EVOLUTION FROM MIS TO DSS: EXTENSION
OF DATA MANAGEMENT TO MODEL MANAGEMENT

by
Robert H. Bonczek
Department of Management
Purdue University
Krannert Graduate School of Management
Krannert Building
West Lafayette, Indiana 47907

Clyde W. Holsapple
Department of Business Administration
University of Illinois
19 Commerce West
1206 S. Sixth Street
Champaign, Illinois 61820

Andrew B. Whinston
Department of Management
Purdue University
Krannert Graduate School of Management
Krannert Building
West Lafayette, Indiana 47907

May 1981

Supported in part by the Army Research Office, Contract No. DA79CO154.

In tracing the evolution of the decision support system (DSS) field from the management information system (MIS) field, several parallels in their early developments are evident. Early literature in the MIS area tended to be anecdotal and definitional. Similarly numerous DSS articles study basic questions confronting the DSS field, such as just what a decision support system is (e.g., [1], [2]). Others discuss specific decision support systems that have been built for particular applications (e.g., [3], [4]). In the 1960s many companies initiated MIS groups, making substantial commitments to create what they considered to be management information systems. Many of these companies deemed their investments to have been well-rewarded, in spite of the fact that debates about the definition of MIS continued. Similarly, an increasing number of companies are forming DSS groups, within and independent of MIS groups.

Over the years numerous generalized software tools appeared as aids for the development of application-specific management information systems. Generalized base management systems (GDBMS) for mainframes, minis and even micros [5] are perhaps the most prominent of these tools. It is reasonable to expect that the next major innovation in the DSS field will be general software tools (beyond GDBMS) that facilitate the construction of application-specific decision support systems. The generic DSS framework detailed in [6] is suggestive of the likely traits of this new class of software tools. In addition, this framework also forms a basis for the comparative study of decision support systems. Following a brief examination of

61

DSS characteristics and the generic framework, we introduce the notion of generalized problem processing systems (GPPS) as tools for building decision support systems. An application independent mechanism for handling application-specific knowledge is then proposed, focusing on the treatment of modeling knowledge.

DSS CHARACTERISTICS

Both MIS and DSS rely upon mechanisms for managing data. However, they differ in terms of the purpose for which data are used. For an MIS application, data are typically used in the context of repetitive, routine transactions and report generations. In contrast, a DSS uses data in responding to ad hoc, exploratory questions of a user who factors the responses into a decision making process. The dividing line between MIS and DSS is not always clear, because a system's data could conceivably be used for both purposes. Nevertheless, the difference in emphasis between MIS and DSS is very clear.

As Figure 1 indicates, a decision support system can generate responses to a user's problem statements by retrieving data, by executing models, or both. Retrieval refers not only to conventional data base retrieval mechanisms, but could also include inferential retrieval [7] which uses formal logic to infer a response on the basis of stored data. Responses can also be generated through the execution of a computational model that utilizes certain stored data as input. This model may be explicitly (i.e., procedurally) specified in the user's problem statement, or it might be invoked in the problem statement, or it may not even be mentioned in the problem statement. In this latter case an appropriate model is selected (or perhaps even formulated) by the decision support system itself. A DSS classification scheme based on these options is detailed in [8]. That is, various decision support systems differ according to which of these options is (or are) employed.

With the first modeling option, a user procedurally states the model's algorithm. This statement may involve extant model building blocks [1] or modules. Under the second alternative, a user is familiar with a collection of pre-specified models available to the DSS. The user selects one of these for execution. Under the third alternative, a user does not directly formulate or select a model; the user may even be unaware that the DSS uses models in generating responses. It is the DSS itself that either selects or formulates a model that is appropriate for solving a stated problem. Present day decision support systems are based on the first two options. It is the third option that is of principal interest in this paper. Clearly this approach requires more intelligence (i.e., artificial intelligence) on the part of a DSS.

Just as a particular management information system is application-specific, a given decision support system is also pertinent for a specific application. A management information system must not be confused with the data base management or file management software package from which it was built. Similarly it is vital not to confuse a decision support system with the software tools from which it is constructed. To the extent that a software tool is general, decision support systems for many different applications can be built from this same software tool. In the following description of the generic DSS framework, various degrees and types of generality are identified.

GENERIC DSS FRAMEWORK

The generic DSS framework [6] maintains that any decision support system can be viewed as having three components. As shown in Figure 2, these are its language system (LS), knowledge system (KS), and problem processing system (PPS). A user

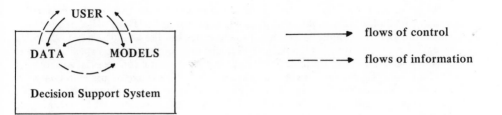

Figure 1

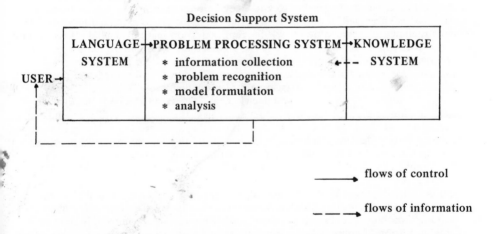

Figure 2

states problems for a DSS to solve by using a language system. A decision support system's KS holds facts about an application area that are relevant to solving problems arising for that application. The problem processor lies at the heart of a DSS, accepting problems represented with the LS and utilizing application-specific knowledge represented in the KS in order to generate information for decision support.

The LS and KS are representation systems. The PPS is the dynamic DSS component; it is a system that displays some behavior. The syntactic and semantic rules of a LS determine the permissible problem statements that can be posed to a DSS. Similarly, a KS is characterized by the facilities it furnishes for the representation and organization of knowledge.

Language systems vary in terms of the level of procedurality that they require for expressing a problem [6]. At one extreme are procedural languages that allow a user to state a problem by specifying the procedural steps (involving retrieval and/or computations) to be used in solving that problem. At the opposite extreme are nonprocedural languages that permit a problem to be specified by merely stating the characteristics of that problem's solution. For example, DISPLAY EPS FOR YEAR = 1983, GROWTH-RATE = .7 AND SHARES = 583400 is a nonprocedural indication of the characteristics of a problem.

Knowledge systems vary not only in terms of the knowledge they contain, but also utilize differing approaches to knowledge representation and organization. If a data base is employed, it may offer hierarchical, network, or extended-network [9] constructs. Other reasonable knowledge representation methods include those from the artificial intelligence area, such as the predicate calculus and production system approaches. Of course, it may be desirable to integrate two or more of these approaches for use in a single knowledge system [7]. The focus of the latter portion of this presentation is upon the treatment of modeling knowledge.

As the software component of a decision support system, a PPS is the formal specification of a DSS's behavior patterns. Clearly, the coding of a PPS depends on the natures of the LS and KS with which the PPS is associated. A problem processor may be more or less general and it may display rudimentary or extensive problem solving abilities. As a minimum any PPS must have the abilities to gather information from a user (expressed via the LS) and from a knowledge system. The latter involves manipulation of data in the KS, while the former ability involves the manipulation of LS expressions. A PPS must also possess the ability to explicitly recognize problems by transforming problem statements into appropriate executable plans of action. A problem processor's problem recognition ability is comparable to the familiar notion of compilation (though it could also be viewed from an interpretive standpoint). A PPS has explicitly recognized a problem when a problem statement has been converted into a detailed procedural specification which, when executed, yields an answer to the problem. For language systems that require a procedural problem statement, the PPS problem recognition ability is at most rudimentary. Nonprocedural problem statements may necessitate a more sophisticated problem recognition ability.

From Figure 1 it is clear that the explicit procedural specification resulting from problem recognition may involve a computational model, as well as retrieval (be it traditional or inferential). If a user directly specifies or selects a model through the LS, then there is no need for the PPS to recognize the modeling problem; the user has already done so. A highly sophisticated problem recognition ability may be required if a PPS must itself select or formulate a model. In the case of model building, the PPS must have a capability beyond information collection and problem recognition abilities. It must have the ability to formulate models, as a service to the problem recognition ability.

Where models are involved, another vital PPS ability is that of analysis. Analysis is the process of interfacing models with data in order to generate some beliefs, facts or expectations. When a PPS has arrived at the explicit recognition of a model and the data that are to be used by it, an analysis mechanism starts and controls the execution. This may merely involve a jump, or it may entail activities such as module loadings and parameter initializations. The precise nature of an analysis mechanism depends largely on how models (modules) are maintained within the DSS. For instance, are they embedded in the PPS code or are they held in the KS?

The foregoing is a brief outline of the generic DSS framework of [6], examining the natures of the three DSS components. Various types of knowledge and language systems were identified. The PPS of a decision support system has several abilities that are useful in problem solving and it must, of course, be consistent with the DSS's language and knowledge systems. This background allows us to consider the notion of a generalized PPS, as a tool for DSS construction, and to subsequently focus on the issue of model management in the context of a DSS built from a GPPS.

GENERALIZED PROBLEM PROCESSOR

If a PPS is not oriented toward a particular application or application area, we shall refer to it as a generalized problem processing system (a GPPS). GPPS code is invariant to changes within an application area and to differences across application areas. In other words a GPPS can be used to build decision support systems in a variety of application areas, without necessitating modifications to the GPPS software. It is this trait that makes a GPPS valuable for the production of customized decision support systems. Problem processor generality implies that the associated KS and LS must also be general in some respects. For instance, if the grammatical structure of a LS is application-specific, changes are likely to be needed in the associated PPS whenever changes are made in the LS grammatical structure to handle a different application. Similarly, the knowledge representation and organization techniques of the KS associated with a GPPS cannot vary from one application to another. Different data manipulation facilities are required for different approaches to knowledge representation and organization. Since these facilities are a part of the GPPS, they cannot be changed from one application to another.

Two different decision support systems (for different applications) built with the same GPPS would exhibit some KS and LS differences. The language systems' lexicons would differ. Though they may employ the same basic grammatical structure, terminal symbols would vary in keeping with the different vocabularies used for distinct applications. Changes in terminal symbols of a LS do not necessarily cause changes in the PPS software. While knowledge systems for a GPPS would utilize the same representation and organization principles, they would vary in terms of how the principles are employed for each application and also in terms of the knowledge contained for each application. GPPS software is unaffected by these types of KS variation.

Using a GPPS, the builder of a DSS for a given application must establish that application's vocabulary, define the application-specific structure of the KS, and initialize (and possibly maintain) the KS contents. Alternatively, a DSS builder could invent and implement a specialized PPS for each application. Between these extremes of GPPS usage and PPS implementation from scratch is the approach of using generalized software packages (a GDBMS for example) in building an application-specific PPS. Comparative advantages of a GPPS approach include easier alteration and maintenance, shorter development time, standardized approach to DSS development, and very likely a lower overall cost. Although full-scale generalized problem processing systems do not exist today, there are some software tools that are steps in the GPPS direction. These include EIS [10], EXPRESS [11], and MDBS.QRS [12]. The former two are intended for specific application areas. The latter is quite general, but does not have the extensive built-in modeling capabilities of the former two.

It is of value to consider the analogy between the role of a GPPS in building a DSS and the role of a GDBMS in MIS construction. The GDBMS software is invariant to changes in application. The data base, its schema, and the application programs or queries (i.e., problem statements) are the only application-specific aspects of a GDBMS-based MIS. In the absence of a GDBMS (or generalized file management software), MIS development tends to be nonstandardized, more time consuming, more difficult to revise, and more expensive. In addition to its generality, the flexibility and ease-of-use provided by a GDBMS for treating various MIS applications are both general, the former are more flexible and easier to use for nontrivial applications. Furthermore there are differences among GDBMS packages in terms of ease-of-use and flexibility.

Flexibility and ease-of-use are also important features for a GPPS and its associated KS and LS. These features should ease the DSS administrator's work in devising, initializing, and revising a DSS. There are many issues connected with providing these features. For instance, does the GPPS have the capacity to handle models as well as ad hoc retrievals? What are the restrictions on selecting or formulating models? Who, or what GPPS mechanism, does the formulating? Is knowledge representation limited to simplistic flat files or is the more facile, flexible network (or even extended-network) approach to schema design supported? It is necessary that a GPPS developer be aware of such questions. Moreover, a GPPS developer should recognize that the key to achieving generality for a problem processor is to allow all application-specific knowledge to be isolated into the KS, where it can be accessed by the GPPS.

GDBMS generality derives from the isolation of application-specific data in a data base, apart from the GDBMS software. We refer to this as environmental data, since it typically describes the state of an application system's environment. In the case of a GPPS, application-specific knowledge consists not only of mundane environmental knowledge (like that handled by a GDBMS) but also of procedural knowledge and meta-knowledge [13]. These latter two refer respectively to application-specific modules (i.e., procedures) and to knowledge about how to use the procedural and environmental knowledge. The remainder of this presentation proposes an approach to representing, organizing and utilizing this modeling knowledge within the context of a GPPS and its associated KS.

KNOWLEDGE SYSTEM DEFINITION LANGUAGE

The broad issue here is how to integrate modeling knowledge and a data base of environmental knowledge into the KS for a GPPS. We commence with a convenient modeling knowledge representation method using Horn clauses. This is illustrated with an inventory application. We then introduce a new data base structuring construct that supports a unified view of modeling and environmental knowledge. That is, it integrates traditional data base structuring and Horn clauses into a single, unified knowledge system definition language (KSDL).

In data base mangement, a Data Definition Language (DDL) is used to specify the structure of the data. This is done by defining indivisible and aggregate units of data and the relationships among these aggregations. The associated data base control system (DBCS) would access the actual data occurrences in the data base through commands that utilize the structure defined in the DDL.

The DDL is a language in the sense that it provides information to the DBCS through established protocols, and the DBCS is able to act on the information received from the compiled DDL. In essence, a sentence in this "language" is parsed, by a special DDL language processor, and the underlying deep structure [6] becomes the input to the DBCS. A similar language must exist for a GPPS, allowing the formal specification of KS structure. This KSDL must possess a DDL as a subset.

One obvious difference between data base and the KS of a DSS is that the latter would contain modeling knowledge as well as environmental knowledge. This leads to two important questions concerning the operation of the PPS of a DSS: how can the input-output requirements of the models be satisfied, using information gleaned from the data base; and how can models (i.e., modules) be combined to produce more structurally complex models?

What is required is a "language" for describing these two interfaces. In [6], the first order predicate calculus is suggested as an appropriate language. Predicate calculus (or formal logic) is a highly descriptive language, i.e., most common relationships and arguments can be expressed naturally in terms of predicate calculus expressions. Furthermore, PPS for predicate calculus knowledge systems exist; they are usually called automatic theorem proving systems [14].

In [6], it is noted that the predicate calculus can naturally address itself to the concerns mentioned above: model representation, analysis and construction of more complex models, and fitting data retrieved from a data base with the formal parameters of the model. However, the structure of predicate calculus expressions required can be limited to a special case referred to as Horn clauses [6]. Such clauses are implications of the form

$$(A_1 \wedge A_2 \wedge \ldots \wedge A_n) \rightarrow B$$

where $\wedge$ is the conjunction operator, and $\rightarrow$ is implication. When such expressions are transformed into *clause form,* for use in an automated theorem prover, the expressions have the simple form of

$$\neg A_1 \vee \neg A_2 \vee \ldots \vee \neg A_n \vee B$$

where $-$ is the negation operator, and V the disjunction operator of the predicate calculus (see [6, 14] for details). It should be noted that the value of n is allowed to be zero, i.e., the Horn clause may simply have the form of a single predicate (B).

The purpose of introducing the Horn clause is to provide a high level representation of modeling knowledge. As a side effect, the Horn clauses provide a convenient method of specifying allowable combinations of modules. This is done in a manner reminiscent of the artificial intelligence technique of state space operators [15], where each operator has a series of "preconditions" associated with it. These preconditions must be satisfied before the operator may be used. Also, the output of the module (operator) can be viewed as "postconditions."

Any predicate calculus expression can be rephrased as a set of one or more Horn clauses. Thus Horn clauses represent a normal form for predicate calculus expressions, i.e., the set of all Horn clauses is identical to the set of predicate calculus expressions. The structure of Horn clauses, however, leads to certain efficiencies in both processing and conceptualization.

It is possible to distinguish among three different types of predicate expressions that will be used in the Knowledge System Definition Language (KSDL). Each record type defined in the static data base (DDL) will represent a predicate symbol; the associated data items define the arguments of the predicate symbol. These predicates shall be referred to as *static* predicates. The second form of predicates will refer to models available for execution by the PPS. The arguments of these predicates will correspond to the formal arguments of the associated procedures (computer programs). Predicates that refer to models shall be called *dynamic* predicates. The final type of predicate is used for inter-model communication. These *parametric* predicates are the connecting links among the different predicate types.

One of the tenets of structured programming and structured design is that communications between procedures should be fully defined, i.e., not obscured by the calling sequences. Following this lead, in the KSDL all Horn clauses are restricted to contain no more than one dynamic predicate per clause, and dynamic predicates may appear only to the left of the implication. In this way it is possible to interpret the remaining predicates as defining the inputs to the procedure (model) if they appear on the left side of the implication, and as defining outputs if they appear on the right side.

It should be clear that this in no way limits the complexity of the kinds of models that can be constructed. Rather, it formalizes the inter-model communication process, and simplifies the model building process, both from the point of view of the user of the DSS, and the PPS itself.

In Figure 3, an example of a data base structure for inventory management is presented. The network data structure keeps track of the items we consume and produce, the quantity on hand of each item, sales information, and bill-of-materials/material requirements planning (MRP) information. The standard network conventions apply here, with record types represented by rectangles, their data item names listed within the rectangle, and set relationships depicted as arrows pointing from the "owner" record type to the "member" record type. The set POST is an example of an N:M set, where each account is influenced by many invoices (potentially), and each invoice may influence several accounts (payable, cash, bad debt, etc.). This extension to the standard network data base definition is described in [9].

A basic model that interfaces with the data base is the EOQ model. EOQ computes the optimal reorder quantity q of item i in period p, given holding costs c_h, ordering costs c_o, and a demand d.

Many other models could be added to this application. An MRP model could be used to compute material requirements. This in turn could be interfaced with the EOQ model to forecast future demand. A linear programming model could be incorporated to determine the "optimal" production strategy for period p; here the MRP and EOQ models would be used to specify some of the constraints for the program. Other models might include a cost-of-goods-sold model and a simulation of future trends in demand and production.

For our inventory problem a set of Horn clauses defining the EOQ model is presented in Figure 4. There are four dynamic predicates (models) defined. EOQ computes the reorder quantity q for item i in period p with inputs of c_o, d and c_h. Model HOLD computes the average holding cost c_h per unit of item i in periods P; the capital letter refers to an array (relation) retrieved from the data base, i.e., all time periods. Model ORDER computes the average ordering costs C for item i in periods P. Finally, REGRESS performs a linear regression on its inputs, and uses the coefficients and the third argument to compute the fourth.

Static predicates include TIME, ITEM, INVOICE and TRANSFQ. The remaining predicates (OC, DMD, HC, O, PC and PQ) are parametric predicates; that is, they define the interfaces among the models, and between each model and the data base. For example, HC is used in clause (2) to define the output of model HOLD; it also

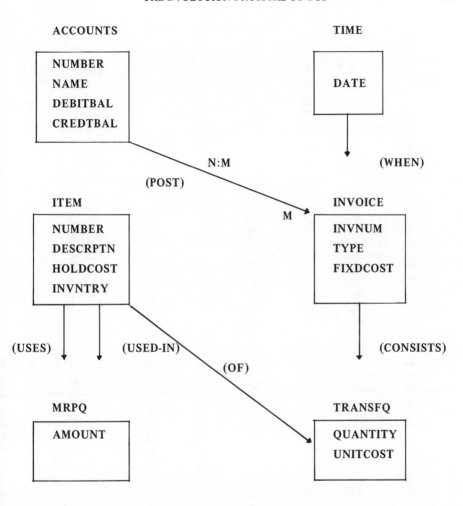

FIGURE 3

$\forall_{co} \forall_i \forall_p \forall_d \forall_{ch} \forall_q [OC(co, i, p) \wedge DMD(d, i, p) \wedge HC(ch, i) \wedge EOQ(co, d, ch, q)] \rightarrow O(i, p, q)$ (1)

$\forall_P \forall_i \forall_x \forall_Y \forall_z \forall_{ch} [TIME(P) \wedge ITEM(i, x, Y, z) \wedge HOLD(P, Y, ch)] \rightarrow HC(ch, i)$ (2)

$\forall_P \forall_x \forall_Y \forall_i \forall_r \forall_s \forall_t \forall_c [TIME(P) \wedge INVOICE(x, \text{"ORDER"}, Y) \wedge ITEM(i, r, s, t) \wedge ORDER(Y, c)]$ (3)
$\rightarrow PC(i, P, C)$

$\forall_i \forall_P \forall_C \forall_p \forall_{co} [PC(i, P, C) \wedge REGRESS(P, C, p, c_o)] \rightarrow OC(c_o, i, p)$ (4)

$\forall_P \forall_x \forall_y \forall_z \forall_Q \forall_i \forall_r \forall_s \forall_t [TIME(P) \wedge INVOICE(x, \text{"SALE"}, y) \wedge TRANSFQ(z, Q) \wedge ITEM(i, r, s, t)]$ (5)
$\rightarrow PQ(i, P, Q)$

$\forall_i \forall_Q \forall_p \forall_d [PQ(i, P, Q) \wedge REGRESS(P, Q, p, d)] \rightarrow DMD(d, i, p)$ (6)

FIGURE 4. Clauses Defining the EOQ Model

appears in clause (1), since this value is used as input to model EOQ.

The clauses "read" quite easily. The first states that "*if* c_O is the ordering cost for item i during period p, *and* d is the demand for item i in period p, *and* c_h is the holding cost for item i, *and* we run EOQ with inputs c_O, d and c_h to obtain output q, *then* the optimal reorder quantity of item i in period p is q." The last clause states that "*if* the past quantities (PQ) of item i during periods P were quantities Q, *and* we regress independent P and dependent Q, and next use the resulting function to forecast demand d in period p, *then* d is the demand for item i in period p. Note the independence of arguments on an inter-clause basis.

Of course, these are not the only possible definitions of the EOQ process. A more general set of constraints might incorporate a test to determine whether the period p is a past or future time; and if it is past time, then skip the forecasting of ordering cost and demand, etc. The clauses presented in the Figure (4), give an indication of how the DSS designer can "program" within the KS to provide the user of the DSS with useful models.

Recall that our purpose was to construct a KSDL along the lines of a DDL for data base management. It would be useful if the DSS designer could use the same linguistic formalism for describing both data and models (i.e., Horn clauses). Of course, as noted above, the record types of data base management are nothing more than the static predicates used in the Horn clauses. Furthermore, it is possible to represent the CODASYL set construction in terms of Horn clauses [6], so that one possible formalism for the KSDL is to express everything in terms of Horn clauses.

This last idea unfortunately would require the DSS designer to become familiar with the Horn clause notation, as well as requiring the development of a new form of analyzer for the KSDL. A better solution would be to augment existing DDL processors, using the established syntax of data base management. In fact, this can be accomplished quite naturally in the present context.

In Figure 5, the "inputs" and "outputs" of the first clause of Figure 4 are diagrammed. The box representing the parametric predicate O is an output, with the arguments labelled within the box itself. And of course the similarity to the network data base diagram of Figure 3 is apparent. In fact, we can diagram the Horn clauses, as we have defined them (with at most a single dynamic predicate per clause), as sets connecting the inputs (owner record types) and outputs (member record types). The interpretation differs from true data base set relationships. This also suggests a formalism for expressing modeling knowledge in our KSDL. We simply adapt the standard set definition formalism, and modify it to include the definition of models. The primary difference is that for models, the arguments of the models must be specified, but this can be handled in a natural manner.

In Figure 6, the KSDL definitions of the CODASYL set USES and the dynamic predicate EOQ are presented side by side for comparison. The fact that EOQ has more than one "owner" declared is not significant; this is allowable under the MDBS implementation [9]. The parametric predicates must also be defined; Figure 7 contrasts the definitions of record type (and static predicate) INVOICE and the parametric predicate DMD.

In clause (5) of Figure 4, there is no dynamic predicate that appears. This clause is simply defining for later use the arrays P and Q for use in clause (6). In this case a null model would be specified in the KSDL. This technique is an important tool for the DSS designer.

Also, model REGRESS is used in two clauses, (4) and (6). Thus it would be defined twice in the KSDL. This will occur often for commonly used routines.

The designer of the DSS can now use the familiar data base constructs to build

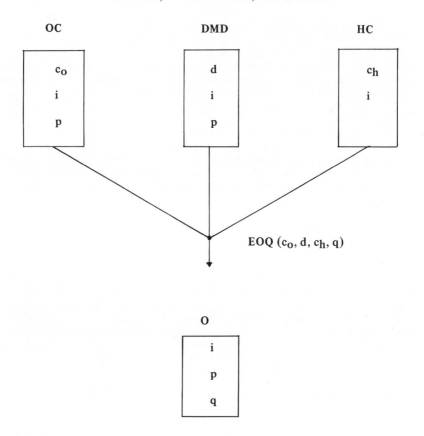

FIGURE 5. Diagram of EOQ-Defining Clause

the KS. The restriction of one model per Horn clause translates itself into having but one "member" type of each dynamic "set." In Figure 8, the entire "knowledge structure" for this DSS is depicted. From such a diagram the DSS designer can evaluate and implement the DSS with ease.

Note that the right hand side of a Horn clause is now viewed as a static predicate. The diagramming technique makes the interpretation of this fact simple: the output of the model can be stored in the data base as a record occurrence. This important aspect of modeling knowledge is thus already within the KSDL formalism.

Other DDL features can be applied to dynamic and parametric predicates. In particular, access and processing protection may be provided through the same security mechanisms inherent in the data base management system. Thus certain users of the DSS may be denied access to models in the same way they are denied access to sensitive data. That both data and models share identical processing procedures with respect to many facets of data management, including security, is an important concept for DSS design and DSS processing.

Furthermore, a dynamic restructuring system (such as [16]) could be used to redefine the models and predicates. For example, if a new forecasting model becomes available, the necessary Horn clauses could be added to the data base to incorporate the model. Also, if the network data structure is dynamically restructured to include new information relevant to the EOQ process, then the definitions can be modified to utilize the additional information.

A GPPS for the KSDL

Consider the operation of a DBCS for a data base. This DBCS would use the structures defined in the DDL to organize its problem solving (retrieval) efforts. In the same way, the PPS of a DSS must use the Horn clauses of the KSDL to organize the invocation and execution of models. There are several ways in which a PPS could perform this task.

For data base management, the DBCS usually analyzes the data structure dynamically. This means that the DBCS has no preconceptions on the form of the data base, or on the allowable solution paths through the data base. PPS model treatment could be organized in the same way. With each problem to be solved, the PPS would attempt to establish all possible solution paths through the KS, including the discovery of Horn clause sequences and the binding of data to models. This approach is quite general; it is also quite cumbersome, especially if the pool of models is large.

The alternate approach is to establish a set of static solution paths that can be accessed as needed. It is possible, within the formalization of predicate calculus, to have such solution paths "parameterized," i.e., a solution path involving models can be specified in terms of the formal parameters of the models, and data values will be substituted at execution time. The mechanism for discovering pre-specified paths of Horn clauses is the same tool that would be used in the ad hoc case, namely some form of automatic theorem prover.

Again by analogy to data base management, pre-stored paths through the data structure would be embedded in applications programs. These programs explicitly establish paths with which they work to produce the required output reports. When models are included, the solution paths incorporate both the models and associated data to provide the desired reports. In essence, this process is a high level form of automatic code generation.

The "reports" required from the pre-specified solution path would themselves be specified as Horn clauses. This is true for ad hoc paths as well. In fact, the existence

SET   USES   AUTO   1:N

OWNER   ITEM

MEMBER   MRPQ, ORDER IS FIFO

MODEL   EOQ (c_o, d, c_h, q)

OWNER OC

OWNER DMD

OWNER HC

MEMBER O

FIGURE 6. KSDL Syntax for Models

RECORD INVOICE

ITEM	INVNUM	INTEGER
ITEM	TYPE	CHARACTER 5
ITEM	FIXDCOST	REAL

PREDICATE DMD

ITEM d	REAL
ITEM i	INTEGER
ITEM P	INTEGER

FIGURE 7. KSDL Syntax for Parametric Predicates

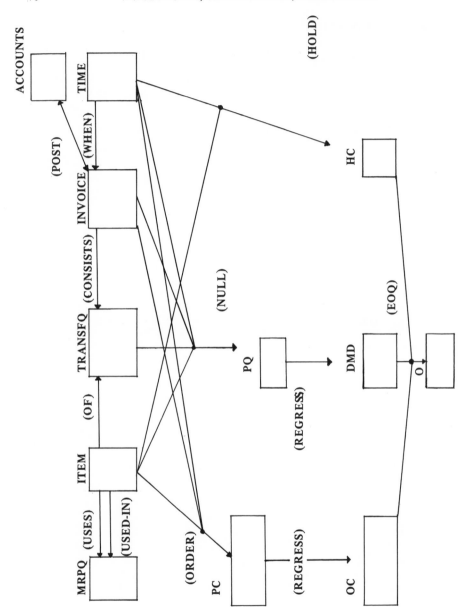

of pre-specified paths does not diminish the necessity of an ad hoc solution capability. This parallels the situation in data base management of report generating programs co-existing with general purpose query retrieval systems. In [6], it is shown that each query in such a retrieval system can itself be represented as a Horn clause. Thus we again see the common unifying theoretical basis of data base management and model management.

A typical "report" would be to determine the optimal reorder quantity. The predicate calculus "command" to do this would be (for item 13006 in 1984)

$$\exists_q \; 0(13006, 1984, q)$$

This "report" could be "programmed" with the KSDL by substituting for the specific year 1984 an existentially quantified variable y:

$$\exists_y \; \exists_q \; 0(13006, y, q)$$

More generally, one would also parameterize the item number as well:

$$\exists_i \; \exists_y \; \exists_q \; 0(i, y, q)$$

Then, a resolution based automatic theorem prover may be used to generate the program.

Part of the allure of a DSS is its ability to answer "what if" questions. In this example, a typical "what if" question might involve demand, e.g., what will be the optimal re-order quantity if demand is 10,000 units? In predicate calculus, this can be expressed as

$$\exists_i \; \exists_y \; \exists_q \; [\, DMD(10000, i, y) \wedge 0(i, y, q)]$$

The "program" for such a report can be obtained by parameterizing the level of demand.

CONCLUSION

This paper addresses a number of important issues concerning the development of DSS. In particular, the importance of understanding and utilizing the underlying frameworks of DSS is noted, and a brief description of a generalized problem processor is presented. Artificial intelligence, and especially formal logic, is used to provide an extension to the data base management technique of data definition, the extension being the treatment of modeling information. The logical equivalence of extended network data structuring and Horn clause representation is described, providing a unified view of knowledge handling.

REFERENCES:

[1] R.H. Sprague, Jr. and H.J. Watson, "Bit by Bit: Toward Decision Support Systems," *California Management Review*, Vol. 12, No. 1, 1979.

[2] P.G.W. Keen, "Decision Support Systems: Translating Analytic Techniques into Useful Tools," *Sloan Management Review*, Vol. 21, No. 2, 1980.

[3] R.A. Seaberg and C. Seaberg, "Computer Based Decision Systems in Xerox Corporate Planning," *Management Science*, Vol. 20, No. 4, 1973.

[4] P. Berger and F. Edelman, "IRIS: A Transaction Based DSS for Human Resources Management," *Data Base*, Vol. 8, No. 3, 1977.

[5] H. Weiss, "Down-Scaling DBMS to the Microworld," *Mini-Micro Systems*, April 1981.

[6] R.H. Bonczek, C.W. Holsapple, and A.B. Whinston, *Foundations of Decision Support Systems*, Academic Press, New York, 1981.

[7] R.H. Bonczek, C.W. Holsapple, and A.B. Whinston, "The Integration of Data Base Management and Problem Resolution," *International Journal of Information Systems*, Vol. 4, No. 2, 1979.

[8] R.H. Bonczek, C.W. Holsapple, and A.B. Whinston, "The Evolving Roles of Models within Decision Support Systems," *Decision Sciences*, April 1980.

[9] *MDBS User's Manual*, Micro Data Base Systems, Inc., Lafayette, Ind., 1980.

[10] *EIS . . . General Overview*, Boeing Computer Services, Morristown, N.J., 1977.

[11] N.C. Shee, et al., "EXPRESS: A Data Extraction, Processing and Restructing System," *Transactions on Data Base Systems*, Vol. 2, No. 2, 1977.

[12] *MDBS-QRS User's Manual*, Micro Data Base Systems, Inc., Lafayette, Ind., 1980.

[13] C.W. Holsapple, "The Knowledge System for a Generalized Problem Processor," working paper, Department of Business Administration, University of Illinois.

[14] C. Chang and R.C. Lee, *Symbolic Logic and Mechanical Theorem Proving*, Academic Press, New York, 1973.

[15] N.J. Nilsson, *Problem Solving Methods in Artificial Intelligence*, McGraw-Hill, New York, 1971.

[16] *MDBS-DRS User's Manual*, Micro Data Base Systems, Inc., Lafayette, Ind., 1980.

DECISION SUPPORT SYSTEMS
M.J. Ginzberg, W. Reitman, E.A. Stohr (editors)
North-Holland Publishing Company
© DSS, 1982

PROTOTYPING FOR DSS: A CRITICAL APPRAISAL
by
John C. Henderson*
Robert S. Ingraham**

*Department of Management
College of Business
Florida State University
Tallahassee, Florida 32306

**Hewlett Packard Co.
Cupertino, California 95014

ABSTRACT

Prototyping or adaptive design has been suggested as an effective approach for developing and implementing DSS. Empirical research has shown this design strategy is effective in establishing meaningful user involvement and high user satisfaction. This paper reveiws the prototyping strategy, examining its use in the design and implementation of a model-based DSS. A comparison with the information require-ments generated by a structured group process indicates that prototyping is a con-vergent design method that may overlook important user information needs.

I. INTRODUCTION

Karl was nervous but ultimately confident. He knew gaining acceptance for his product innovation, a new health food oriented breakfast cereal, was not going to be easy. The Executive Committee, particularly, the Vice-President of Marketing, had become increasingly wary of "innovative" products. The procedures for a cost/benefit analysis had tightened, requiring even higher hurdles to jump.

Karl gave his presentation, and waited for the inevitable question. "Are you sure this will sell?" He responded with results of interviews with leading market analysts and projected sales figures. These "facts" clearly demonstrated the potential profits of this new breakfast cereal. There was silence. Finally, the Vice-President of Market-ing said, "Well, let me taste it." Karl smiled, and knew he had the battle won.

Rarely are decisions made relating to product innovations without a "taste" test. The risks are too high. There are too many questions, too much to learn. Many com-petent managers simply will not commit venture capital without some "hands on" experience. Thus, we see engineers developing pilot plants to test the commercial feasibility of new processes, and marketing research groups running well-designed market tests on new products. Ultimately, decisions are based on the actual experi-ence with the new process or product. How good does it taste?

And yet, as Management Information Systems designers, we pursue a quite dif-ferent strategy. Following the concept of the design life cycle, we often invest close to 70% of the total project costs before any actual experience with the system is gained. The early experiences that are gained normally involve "testing" by analysts. Usage by system clients does not occur until the last stages of the design process.

This design strategy involves a fundamental assumption; the requirements of the system can be predetermined. Thus, we have seen keen interest in information requirements definition (IRD) in the last decade. Traditionally, IRD is accomplished by a combination of logical analysis and investigation of user information processing behavior. We determine the requirements of an accounts receivable information system by examining accounting procedures and talking to our experienced accountants.

But where does this approach leave us with Decision Support Systems (DSS)? DSS are systems designed to *enhance* the decision processes of managers faced with ill-structured decisions. By definition, we do not, perhaps cannot, completely understand the user's needs. As a result, we must explicitly acknowledge the role of learning in our design strategy. That is, we predict that as part of our design and implementation effort the user will "learn" about his/her problem or environment and, thereby, identify new and unanticipated information needs.

Further, since we are unsure of our final objectives, we must admit we are taking a significant risk. We may be designing a system that will be ineffective, perhaps unused. Thus, to gain resources to build our systems, we must seek venture capital.

Generally DSS designers have recognized this circumstance calls for a departure from the traditional design strategy. The strategy suggested as most appropriate is called prototyping or adaptive design. This paper reviews the concept of prototyping, presents a DSS design effort (a case) in which prototyping was used and discusses the results raising some issues of concern regarding this approach.

II. PROTOTYPING: AN ALTERNATIVE STRATEGY

Ness once commented to the effect that design strategies should be based on the principle that 80% of our ideas are bad. The key to success is to spend 80% of our resources on those 20% of the ideas that are good. He suggests (11) a design approach called middle-out which attempts to quickly establish a working model or prototype of a system or problem. Exhaustive analysis of user requirements is avoided as is extensive system design and documentation. Efficiency goals are replaced by effectiveness goals. One doesn't really care how it is done, simply that it is done.

Middle-out design was an early framework for prototyping. Current work on this design strategy is found under several terms such as adaptive design (10) or evolutionary design (1) and seems to suggest five primary features of prototyping. First, learning is explicitly integrated into the design process. This goal is normally accomplished by designing systems in an iterative fashion. A prototyped system is built and placed in the hands of the user. The user evaluates this "system," determines necessary enhancements and sends it back to the analyst. The analyst updates the prototype, returning it to the user for more "commercial" tests. Thus, the designer expects to err, but attempts to learn as much as possible from such errors.

Berrisford and Wetherbe (4), Bally, et al (3) and others contrast the role of learning in prototyping with that of learning in the traditional design approach. They note that the traditional approach is based on a sequential, single iteration of the design life cycle. Recycling or looping back to early stages implies *poor* performance. The key to success is to do it right the first time through. Obviously this greatly reduces the opportunity to apply lessons learned during latter stages, i.e., conversion, to early stages, i.e., user requirements. Prototyping assumes one will iterate, learning from actual usage, and thus remove the pressure to "do it right" the first time.

Secondly, a key criterion associated with prototyping is time between iterations. The feedback or iterations must be relatively fast. This criterion results from basic understanding as to how to support learning. That is, good, timely feedback is a prerequisite to effective learning processes.

Third, involvement by users is a key feature. Prototyping assumes that the user must actively participate in the design. This requirement stems from a need to use their expertise in the design effort as well as recognizing that successful implementation will be more easily achieved with active involvement.

Fourth, the initial prototype must be "low" cost. It must fall below the minimum threshold for capital outlay justification. The development of a prototype is a risky decision, particularly for a DSS. And yet, the benefits of DSS are often "soft" relating to issues such as "improved decision making" or "better understanding." In such circumstances, a high initial investment may result in a decision *not* to proceed.

Finally, prototyping essentially bypasses the life cycle stage of information requirements definition. Rather, it evolves requirements via the user learning process. The strategy assumes requirements are only partially known and attempts to clarify needs by actively involving the user in a low cost, fast feedback development process.

III. PROTOTYPING: A CASE STUDY

Decision Support Systems are designed to help managers cope with semi-structured decision tasks. This means that the manager is faced with a problem in which (1) relevant information for decision making is unavailable, and/or (2) alternatives are unknown, and/or (3) appropriate values for making a choice are unknown. The purpose of a DSS is to facilitate the judgement processes as one attempts to contend with these unknowns. In this application, the primary uncertainty centers around the values or priorities used to allocate funds.

The Franklin County, Ohio, Mental Health Board allocates close to 20 million dollars per year to community mental health programs. With increasing costs and inflation, coupled with possible decreases in federal and state funds, the MH Board faces a serious allocation problem. For the most part, the alternatives are well known. They are the various treatment programs offered by agencies throughout the county. Further, the data base for allocations is fairly well established. A history of facility utilization, unit costs and demand provides a good data base for allocation planning. The critical uncertainty is the weights or priorities to give any particular program or client. For example, should the county continue to fund children's programs at current levels even if that might mean substantial reduction in care for the elderly? Obviously, setting these priorities involves human judgement. To better support this judgement process, a multicriteria allocation planning model was developed to provide an interactive, model-based DSS.

The general structure of the system is shown in Figure 1. Essentially it has three components: a model coordination system, a data management system and a DSS reporting system. The model coordination system links the cost data and utilization data from the county operating information system to a model generation component. This component generates a model in a form that could be solved by the model execution module.

The model itself is a multicriteria allocation model that minimizes the distance for an "ideal" goal attainment. The ideal goal attainment is generated by maximizing single goal allocation models, one for each of the goals represented. The solution of these models provides both an upper limit or idealistic goal attainment as well as a lower bound on goal attainment (i.e., lowest given the existing constraints). Obviously, since conflicts exist between goals, the ideal goal attainment can not be achieved. Rather, the model considers tradeoffs between goals based on the priorities assigned to goals and the technological and economic relationships represented in the constraint set. More formally, the model appears as:

$$\text{Min } Z = \sum_{k=1}^{p} \left| Z_k^* - Z_k(x) \right|$$

s.t. $x \in Fd$

where Z_k^* = ideal goal attainment for K^{th} goal.

$Z_k(x)$ = K^{th} goal as a function of the decision variables, $\underline{X}$.

X = decision variable indicating the dollars allocated to a particular agency for a particular service provided to a given client type.

Fd = feasible region formed by economic, legal and managerial policy constraints.

After execution, the data management component uses the solution data base to create several application data bases. In general, the application data bases involve some type of aggregation. For example, one such data base aggregates service levels across an agency for each goal. This approach provides for increased efficiency, and thus, faster response time. For the most part these data bases were generated for information needs that were high priority and reasonably stable. Of course, the original solution data base is accessible if an information request is incompatible with these application data bases.

This component also manages the merging of label data bases, historical solution data bases and geographic or demographic data bases. Thus, the solution generated by the model can easily be combined with contextual information to increase the overall effectiveness of the reporting system. Further, changes to the contextual data bases or to the model are interdependent so that the system can easily be modified during the prototyping process.

One important feature of this component is that it allows the user or analyst to process large transaction data bases in a traditional MIS mode. Since the data used to estimate unit cost, demand and so on are often the center of controversy during implementation, this is an important feature. The impact of this capability will be discussed in Section IV.

Finally, the DSS reporting control (currently consisting of over thirty separate programs) generates management reports ranging from goal attainment to detailed allocations. In general, these programs were developed in response to requests for information by users during the prototyping effort. Programs normally consist of 50-100 lines of code (written in SAS) and average about 1 hour for development and testing. The use of the high level languages coupled in model structure or data management allows new reports to be integrated into the system easily and efficiently.

The model-based DSS is designed to allow the decision makers to investigate the impact of changing their priorities. The overall process used in implementing this DSS is shown in Figure 2. First, the Board held a series of meetings to debate and clarify its basic purpose or mission. Issues such as its role relative to private sector service providers, legal mandates and other global issues were debated.

As a result of these discussions, the Board chose to conceptualize their mental health system using the Balanced Service System[2] (BSS) Model. This model views emotional disability as a dysfunctional state that is often reoccurring in nature. Treatment

[2]The version of the Balance Service System Model used in this study was developed by the staff of the Franklin County, Ohio, Community Health Board. Those interested can contact Franklin County for a more detailed description.

programs are defined by the environment in which they are provided and their basic goals of the service treatment. In the simple model, environments are protective (e.g., a hospital), supportive (e.g., an outpatient center), and natural (e.g., community work program).

Service classes are crisis stabilization (emergency room treatment), growth (skill development) or sustenance (maintaining social skills). This simple model, shown in Figure 3, provides a basis to articulate goals. For example, the level of service in each cell may be a goal. "Balancing" service across environments may be a goal. Further, the more elaborate BSS model used by the MH Board also considers client groups (e.g., children) and geographic and demographic based goals. Hence, the classic issues of equity in the public sector are directly addressed.

Finally, the Board considered tradeoffs between three fundamental disability areas: Mental Health, Mental Retardation and Substance Abuse (primarily drug abuse). Thus, in this study the Board formulated 27 primary goals; the amount of service in each cell at the simple Balance Service System Model (Figure 3) for each disability type. Each goal was measured in terms of the units of service actually funded or purchased."[3]

Having formulated the goals, the decision makers prioritize the goals, process the multiobjective allocation planning model and then evaluate the resulting goal attainments (Figure 2). The allocation model generates the optimal allocation of resources (i.e., units purchased) given these priorities and given system constraints (e.g., financial limits, capacity limits, legal constraints, federal matching requirements and so on). Thus, the evaluations are made within a consistent feasible framework.

The prototyping effort concentrated on two aspects of the system; the information provided to the decision makers and the characteristics of the overall DSS. The latter issue was directed toward achieving a system that could eventually be used by nontechnical decision makers. It was assumed that the model was appropriately defined. As will be discussed in the next section, the user experiences clearly indicated this assumption was false.

Most of the components of the DSS were written in a high level, analytic language (SAS). This permitted both easy adaption of the system and allowed a design that was very modularized. The modularity created the system flexibility necessary to support a prototyping effort. That is, changes could be made to one component of the system without affecting other components thereby minimizing the time between interactions.

IV. RESULTS AND DISCUSSION

This study involved the actual design and implementation of a model-based DSS.[4] There were 5 decision makers involved; 2 Board members and 3 staff members. The Board members were chosen because of their key positions on the planning committee and because they were willing participants in the prototyping effort. The staff members provided in-depth experience with both service providers and the existing

[3]It is important to realize these goals were formulated by Board members participating in group discussions. Actual historical data coupled with demand forecasts were used to evaluate the "need" within cells and the various unit costs, available capacity and so on.

[4]Those involved clearly understood that this version of the system was a prototype and therefore might need alteration. As it was quite early in the budget cycle, there was time to incorporate recommended changes. The subsequent version was actually used by the Board to help set priorities.

system. The prototyping effort lasted approximately 4 months. Two months were spent developing the initial system, and two months conducting the adaptive design process with the users.

Each individual functioned separately attempting to reach a "best" priority profile. There were no time pressures. In fact, some decision makers spent extended periods of time evaluating the output. The initial set of reports (and their information items) were determined using unstructured interviews with both staff and Board members. In the spirit of prototyping, an attempt to exhaustively enumerate and validate information needs was avoided. Rather, interviews were used to establish a reasonable starting point.

Further, these decision makers were asked to assume their decisions would be implemented. Clearly, any recommendation by the planning members would have to be ratified by the Board as a whole. Still, the decision makers clearly understood that the final DSS system would actually be used to support the allocation planning process.

An iteration of the prototyping effort involved a decision maker reviewing the output of the DSS, selecting a new set of priorities and then evaluating the merits of the information provided for goals by the DSS. The evaluation consisted of answering the following questions:

1. I would like to see the following new information and/or report format changes.

2. I would like to make the following suggestions/criticisms about the process and the system under development.

3. Rank the reports you used in order of their usefulness to you in making your decision (from most important to least important).

4. The following reports need *not* be provided.

In addition, at the end of the prototyping effort the decision makers were asked the extent to which they were satisfied with the information on reports they were receiving and the extent to which the allocation model generated a solution they found unacceptable.

Finally, after each individual had finally terminated his or her interaction with the system, a structured group process (a nominal group process with only one vote) was held to determine if any additional information might be appropriate. Following this meeting each decision maker was asked to reevaluate the existing reports.

THE EVALUATION OF INFORMATION REQUIREMENTS

The initial set of reports provided to the decision makers is shown in Table 1a. Those reports requested by users during the process are shown in Table 1b. The number of iterations executed for each decision maker ranged from 2 to 9. Analyzing report usage, it was found that all requests for new information and for deletion of existing reports were completed in less than four steps. Table 2 shows the reports used by each decision maker in each situation (the letters correspond to those shown in Table 1).

The intervention of a group process had a significant effect. Table 3 shows the rank ordering of useful reports for each decision maker at the beginning of the prototyping effort, at the final iteration and after the group process. In addition new requests for information surfaced during the group process. These requests are summarized in Table 4.

DISCUSSION OF INFORMATION REQUIREMENTS EVALUATION

Several issues are raised by these results. First, the users appeared to rapidly converge to a small number of reports. This suggests a strong learning curve effect and is consistent with psychological research relating to the behavior of individuals that experience information overload (7).

The possible effect of this early convergence is also illustrated by the new information generated as a result of a group process. The group process promoted a more divergent, creative need generation process resulting in new information needs being identified. A conflict, however, exists in that the subject indicated *satisfaction* with the information they were receiving at the conclusion of the prototyping effort. Thus we see prototyping leads to a quick convergence and fosters user satisfaction *but* it may converge so quickly that important information requirements will go unnoticed.

These results also illustrate one of the major difficulties in designing a DSS—individual differences among decision makers. No one report was requested by every decision maker. Some wanted much more detail than others. Some wanted graphics while others did not. In fact, there were no reports identified as favorable by all decision makers.

Finally, the effect of a group process is also seen in terms of the information individuals viewed as important. Table 3 provides the report ranking at the final step after the group process. Note that many changes in both ranking and amount of information are shown. It is not clear, however, if these individuals would actually continue to use these new reports during their decision making processes.

We can also see the effect of the group process by examining the report rankings summed across individuals before and after the group process (Table 5). Of course, summing rank orders requires the rather dubious assumption that the ranks are intervally scaled. Still, even when viewed cautiously, the change in the perceived usefulness of some reports (e.g., SERENVT, HISTCATH, and PASTSTEP) is dramatic.

Clearly, the debates and rationalizations of a peer group have significant impact on information usage. This result has been demonstrated many times. The important question is the impact of a converging design technique, often used at the individual level, such as prototyping. We simply do not know if the final result of prototyping is, in fact, a "best" system definition.

EVOLUTION OF SYSTEM CHARACTERISTICS

Several basic changes in the system design occurred as a result of the prototyping effort. First, the use of IBM Command Language was increased. This allowed the system to coordinate and sequence program modules without the use of a technical intermediary. For example, several of the modules created data bases that were required as input to other modules. The creation of an overall executive function using macro command statements allow this type of coordination to become transparent to the user.

The second set of changes focused on the interaction with the model. Perhaps the most significant contribution of the design effort was in terms of evaluating and enhancing the allocation model. As the decision makers examined solutions, they raised issues that required adapting the basic allocation model. Some changes represented Board policy such as the inclusion of minimum service allocation levels for specific classes at agencies. Other changes reflected legal or financial relationships not previously recognized. For example, the model had to be adapted to account for block grants and alternative sources of funding.

The important result was the need to link the matrix generation module used to formulate the model with the operating information system of the mental health system. It was not sufficient to assume that a set of parameters could be abstracted from this large data base and used throughout the decision making process. Rather, the political consequences of an allocation often resulted in a need to run an alternatively structured model. This in turn required accessing the transaction data base for new parameter estimates, input data and so on. Thus the overall structure of the DSS had to be expanded to permit, at a minimum, an intermediary to easily link to a fundamental transaction data base. In this sense, the distinction between a model-based DSS and a Data-Oriented DSS (2) becomes quite vague.

Finally, the notion discussed by Brooks (6) proved appropriate for this project. Brooks distinguishes between the effort to develop a program, a programming system, a programming product and a fully integrated system product. He notes that the effort involved is nonlinear as one moves towards developing an integrated system product. This proved true in this study. Developing the basic set of programs to generate a solution and produce reports was fairly easy. This is particularly true given the use of a language such as SAS. However, creating an interactive, maintainable total system that could allow for updating a complex optimization model, support individual or group processes and link to a transaction data base proved much more complex. The prototyping effort clearly helped to determine the requirements of such a system. However, it is *not* clear that it would be cost-effective to continue using this approach to actually design and implement the more complex integrated programming systems product.

V. CONCLUSION

Clearly, one has to be quite careful in drawing a conclusion from a single case study. However, several practical research questions have been raised in this study that require further attention. First prototyping appears to be a highly convergent design process. As would be expected from the research on human behavior and learning theory, such a process will create high user satisfaction. However, this case study suggests that such convergence may be detrimental in that significant information needs may be missed. In essence, we may be propagating a status-quo which is sub-optimal.

Secondly, the influence of individual difference is strong. An issue in DSS design using prototyping or adaptive processes is how to contend with this circumstance. Again, by focusing on an individual we may create a more "accessible" system in that the features reflect the biases of the individual. However, we also lose the potential creativity associated with effective group design processes.

Finally, we note that prototyping did provide an effective mechanism to develop user insight into a complex model-based DSS. However, the result is a need for an integrated programming system product that combines both data oriented features with model-based features. At this juncture, we are impressed with the capability of the prototyping effort to *define these requirements* but are pessimistic as to its effectiveness in actually pursuing the development of an integrated system product. In essence we suggest the last interaction in a prototyping effort may, in fact, be a very traditional design process. The benefit in prototyping is the availability of a crude but usable immediate system that can support the user during the extended system development life cycle.

Figure 1

Overview for Mental Health DSS

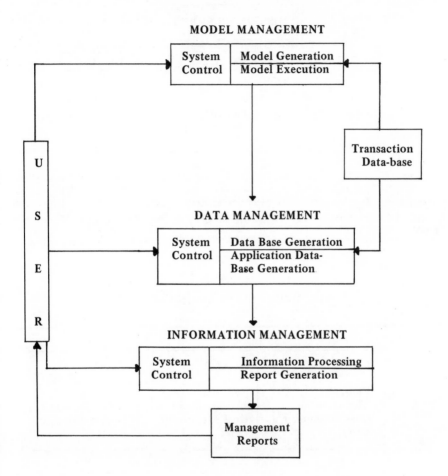

Figure 2

Planning Process for Allocation of Funds

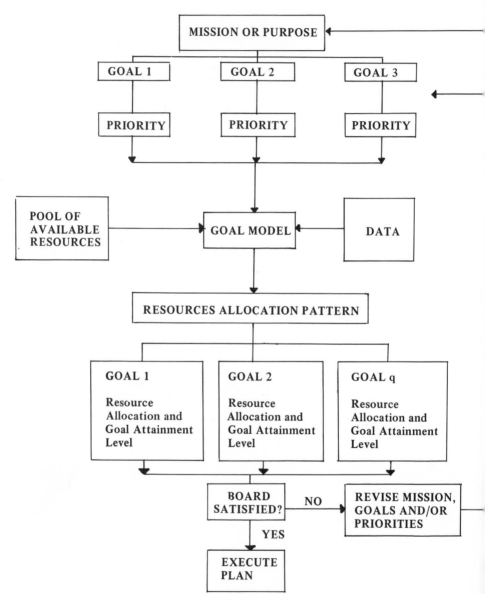

Figure 3
BSS Model

	Protective	Supportive	Natural
Crisis Stablization			
Growth			
Sustenance			

Table 1a

Initial Reports Provided by DSS

a. GOALPLOT: presents goal attainments

b. SUMMARY: total dollars by source of funds, environment and service

c. DETAIL: total dollars as in SUMMARY for each agency

d. PERIDEAL: comparison of goal attainments to maximum level of service

e. PERCENT: goal attainment as percent of need

f. PLOTPCNT: graphical presentation of PERCENT

Table 1b

Additional Reports as a result of
the Prototyping Process

g. SERENVT: breakdown of dollars and units by detailed BSS model

h. CATCH: proposed dollars and units for geographical region

i. PASTSTEP: comparison of current solution with previous solution

j. HISTORY: last year dollars and units by detailed BSS model

k. HISTCATH: last year dollars and units by detailed BSS model by region

l. UNITCOST: trace calculations for unit costs

m. IDLPCT: current solution as percent of maximum service level

Table 2

Usage of Reports by Decision Maker

Number of Steps

	1	2	3	4	5	6	7	8	9	10	Group
1	a f b c d e	a b c d									a f c h j b
2	a f b c d e	f	f g	f g							k i c b j
3	a f b c d e	a c d e h	a c d e h	a d e h i	a d e h i	a d e h i	a d e h i				b h j f k i l
4	a f b c d e	a f b j c k d e	a b g j k	a i b g h k	a i b g j k	a i b g j k	a i b g j k				l i a
5	a f b c d e	a f	a f	a f	a f	a f	a f	a f	a f		f c a k j i b

Decision Maker

Table 3

Preferred Reports by Decision Makers

Subject No.	Beginning Reports	Last Step Reports	After Group Reports
1	GOALPLOT	GOALPLOT	GOALPLOT
	SUMMARY	DETAIL	PLOTPCNT
	DETAIL	SUMMARY	DETAIL
	PERCENT	PERIDEAL	CATCH
	PERIDEAL		HISTORY
	PLOTPCNT		SUMMARY
2	GOALPLOT	PASTSTEP	PASTSTEP
	SUMMARY	GOALPLOT	GOALPLOT
	DETAIL	SERENVTS	UNITCOST
	PERCENT	HISTORY	
	PERIDEAL	HISTCATH	
	PLOTPCNT	SUMMARY	
3	GOALPLOT	PASTSTEP	PASTSTEP
	SUMMARY	PERCENT	HISTCATH
	DETAIL	PERIDEAL	HISTORY
	PERCENT	GOALPLOT	SUMMARY
	PERIDEAL	CATCH	UNITCOST
	PLOTPCNT	PLOTPCNT	CATCH
			PLOTPCNT

Table 3 (continued)
Preferred Reports by Decision Makers

Subject No.	Beginning Reports	Last Step Reports	After Group Reports
4	GOALPLOT	PLOTPCNT	HISTCATH
	SUMMARY	SERENVTS	PASTSTEP
	DETAIL		DETAIL
	PERCENT		SUMMARY
	PERIDEAL		HISTORY
	PLOTPCNT		
5	GOALPLOT	GOALPLOT	PLOTPCNT
	SUMMARY	PLOTPCNT	GOALPLOT
	DETAIL		HISTORY
	PERCENT		PASTSTEP
	PERIDEAL		SUMMARY
	PLOTPCNT		DETAIL
			HISTCATH

Table 4

Major Changes Resulting from Group Process

1. Enlarge model to include the effects of another source of funds.

2. Adjust model to include the effects of block grants.

3. Add core constraints to service levels.

4. Change core location constraint to core location and source of funds constraints.

5. Change core location constraints to reflect individual differences instead of an across the board, 80% of last year's allocation figure.

6. Drop migration adjustments out of the model.

7. Change catchment area goals to an artificial reporting category only.

Note: these changes to the model were also reflected in requests for additional information items

Table 5

Summary of Preferred Reports across Decision Makers

Favorite Reports

After Step Process			After Group Process	
Report	Score		Report	Score
GOALPLOT	19		PASTSTEP	24
PLOTPCNT	19		HISTORY	20
PASTSTEP	14		GOALPLOT	19
SERENVTS	11		HISTCATH	18
PERIDEAL	9		DETAIL	14
SUMMARY	7		SUMMARY	14
DETAIL	6		PLOTPCNT	14
PERCENT	6		UNITCOST	8
HISTORY	4		CATCH	6
HISTCATH	3		PERIDEAL	2
CATCH	3		SEREMVTS	2
UNITCOST	0		PERCENT	1

REFERENCES:

[1] Alavi, Maryam and Henderson, John C., "An Evolutionary Strategy for Implementing a Decision Support System." Forthcoming in *Management Science.*

[2] Alter, S.A., *Decision Support Systems: Current Practice and Continuing Challenges.* Reading, Massachusetts: Addison-Wesley Publishing Company, 1980.

[3] Bally, Laurent; Brittan, John; and Wagner, Karl H., "A Prototyping Approach to Information System Design and Development." *Information and Management,* (Vol. 1). 1977, pp. 21-26.

[4] Berrisford, T.R., and Wetherbe, J.C., "Heuristic Development: A Redesign of System Design." *MIS Quarterly,* (Vol. 3, No. 1). March 1979, pp. 11-19.

[5] Boland, R.J., Jr. "The Process and Product of System Design." *Management Science,* (Vol. 24, No. 9). May 1978, pp. 887-898.

[6] Brooks, Frederick P., Jr. *The Mythical Man-Month: Essays on Software Engineering.*

[7] Chervany, Norman L., and Dickson, Gary W. "An Experimental Evaluation of Information Overload in a Production Environment." *Management Science,* (Vol. 20, No. 10). June 1979, pp. 1335-1344.

[8] Hayes, R.H. and Nolan, R.L. "What Type of Corporate Modeling Functions Best." *Harvard Business Review.* May-June, 1974, pp. 102-112

[9] Keen, Peter G.W. and Scott Morton, Michael S., *Decision Support System: An Organizational Perspective.* Reading, Massachusetts: Addison-Wesley Publishing Company.

[10] Keen, Peter G.W. and Gambino, T.J., "Building a Decision Support System: The Mythical Man-Month Revisited." To appear in *Building Decision Support Systems.* J.F. Bennett (ed.). Addison-Wesley Publishing Company.

[11] Ness, D., "Interactive Systems: Theories on Design." *Joint Wharton/DNR Conference-Interactive Information and DSS.* Dept. of Decision Sciences, The Wharton School. University of Pennsylvania. November 1975.

[12] Urban, G.L. and Karash, R., "Evolutionary Model Building." *Journal of Marketing Research,* (Vol. 8). February 1971.

DECISION SUPPORT SYSTEMS
M.J. Ginzberg, W. Reitman, E.A. Stohr (editors)
North-Holland Publishing Company
© DSS, 1982

OPTIMIZATION IN
INTERACTIVE PLANNING SYSTEMS
by
E. Gerald Hurst, Jr.
Michel R. Kohner

Department of Decision Sciences
The Wharton School
University of Pennsylvania
Philadelphia, PA 19104

ABSTRACT

In the past decade interactive planning systems have become convenient and widely available and are now used on the planning problems of hundreds of organizations. These systems are used to relate the important controllable and external factors to the performance measures of the organization, obtain appropriate data, and perform sensitivity analyses on the effects of various values of the input factors. This paper describes a method for finding the optimal value of a selected result variable and the related controllable variables. The issues involved in optimizing a formal planning model are presented and a working prototype system is demonstrated.

INTRODUCTION

10 PRINT "WHAT ARE XMIN AND XMAX",

20 INPUT X1, X2

30 FOR X=X1 TO X2 STEP (X2−X1)/10

40 PRINT X, (any function of X)

50 NEXT X

60 GO TO 10

This six-line BASIC program can quickly be used to find the optimal value of any function of one variable, no matter how complicated the function. The strength of this simple program comes from the human-machine partnership. By using a human to review its output and formulate subsequent input, this program illustrates the problem solution power obtained by combining the strengths of human and computer.

The program is a simple example of a Human Aided Optimization system [7]. HAO systems have three essential characteristics:

1. An interactive computer system. The computer system is used in a hands-on fashion by a human who inputs requests, data, and other items of use to the system, and gets an immediate response.

2. Optimum-seeking methods. These methods include a measure of performance or figure of merit and some mechanism for finding a "better" value of this measure based on values already computed. This optimizing component makes HAO a subset of decision support systems.

3. Human-machine partnership. The human is an integral part of the solution process, not just a solution starter and stopper. In addition to providing answers to questions from the human, an HAO system asks the human for aid at various stages in the process — defining the problem, choosing subproblems of interest, reviewing intermediate solutions, and resetting constraints, for example.

Any system used for realistically complex problems will have additional features which help the human and the machine communicate. These include:

1. Graphical output, including color, as well as high speed alphanumeric displays.

2. Some form of graphical input, whether touch panel, light pen, track ball, or another form which makes it easy for a human to input data.

3. High-speed intelligent terminals which do some processing before the large computer receives data, or format output after computer processing is done.

4. High level, natural, or special purpose languages, either designed specifically for HAO, or problem-oriented languages to which an optimization option has been added.

A conference on HAO was held in August 1980 at The Wharton School. A number of systems which exploit the principle are available in both commercial and experimental prototypes. Application areas include vehicle routing [3, 9, 10], facility location, scheduling, military flight path selection [13], and pattern packing.

An example of wide-spread commercial use of the principles of HAO is in truck routing. At least 3 different commercial systems have been installed in a number of companies [3]. Typically, a dispatcher interacts with a graphics terminal to prepare schedules and routes which respond to the market needs of the moment. Another more theoretical area in which the human-machine interaction has been widely used is in multicriteria decision making. Here the computer is used to keep track of the preferences as expressed by the human, and to propose new optima based on these preferences.

HAO use appears especially promising in planning problems. Typical planning problems are characterized by unique situation knowledge held by the human planners, complicated combinations of alternative decisions which are difficult to explore exhaustively, and one or more measures of performance by which the alternatives can be evaluated and compared.

Even though planning systems represent an area of high potential for HAO, today there is apparently only one commercial planning system with an optimization option [12]. In addition, one prototype optimizer was developed but never released for public use [5], and at least one in-house planning sytem was built with optimization capability [4].

The current paper presents an expansion and recent re-implementation of the prototype documented in [5], as described more fully in [8]. In the remainder of the paper general characteristics of planning systems are discussed, the desired characteristics of an optimizer for planning system are presented, and a description of the implemented system is given. After an example problem is described, the system is used to find the optimal solution to this problem. The paper closes with a brief discussion of the other advanced features of the prototype system.

PLANNING SYSTEMS

A planning system is used to represent and manipulate models and data appropriate to strategic planning decisions. The availability and characteristics of different planning systems have changed rapidly since they were first introduced in 1967 [2, 6]. There are now approximately 50 different commercial planning systems used in hundreds of organizations. While the system capabilities vary, there are several characteristics which most possess.

Modeling Language

All planning systems have a language in which the unique structure of the planning problem is represented. The ability to custom build the structure of the problem distinguishes these systems from earlier planning software in which the structure was fixed and the user could specify only data values.

In the modeling language, the user describes the structure of the planning problem in the form of a series of computer statements which relate both controllable and external input variables to the output variables considered important. The system takes the supplied values of the input variables and computes the values of the output variables which result. The human knows the content of the model, having supplied it; to the planning system, the model is a black box which computes values of output variables from the values of input variables. Analytical knowledge of the model, if any, resides solely with the human.

Report Generation

Planning systems also have the ability to generate reports. This is done in several ways:

1. Standards reports — The format of the report is fixed; the user selects only the variables included. "What if" and other standard analyses are usually presented in this way.

2. Model parameters — Reports are formatted by setting parameters in the model or by using a special version of a model for generating the report.

3. Report language — A special language, different from the modeling language, is

used to format reports; the variables included and their presentation form are both selected.

4. Graphical reports — Input assumptions and results are presented graphically, either on standard alphanumeric terminals or on special graphics terminals. The options include:

    (a) Variables plotted against time;
    (b) Variables plotted against other variables, as in a scatter diagram;
    (c) Probability distributions, in either histogram or cumulative form.

Analysis Capabilities

The analysis options typically available in planning systems are:

1. Case analysis — The ability to evaluate outcomes for a given set of input values.

2. Parametric analysis (what if . . .) — The ability to vary a set of input values and observe the effect on the outcomes. All planning systems have this capability; it is the most often used analysis option.

3. Sensitivity analysis — An organized version of "what if" analysis, in which one or more input variables take on different values and the effect on the result variables is explored.

4. Break-even analysis (how get ... .) — The ability to find the value of an input variable which yields a desired outcome. This is also known as management by objectives, target value analysis, or goal seeking in some planning systems.

5. Impact analysis — The ability to learn for a chosen result variable all the input variables which affect its value, and, for those which do, the amount of change in the result caused by, say, 1% change in the input value. When this option is available on a planning system, its popularity is second only to "what if" analysis.

6. Data analysis — The ability to input historical data and manipulate it into a forecast suitable for direct input to the model.

7. Comparison and consolidation — The ability to compare the results of two or more runs made with different input assumptions, or to compare predicted with actual results, or to consolidate results from different model runs.

8. Command sequences — The ability to write, execute, and save for later use a regularly executed series of analysis and report commands. This capability permits the user to build special-purpose analysis options from the primitive analysis operations available in the planning system.

In addition to these basic capabilities which are available on most planning systems, two advanced capabilities are being introduced.

1. Risk analysis — The ability to determine the effects of randomness in the input

variables on the potential outcomes, usually by Monte Carlo simulation. Several systems have the rudimentary ability to perform this analysis, usually by specifying randomness through the variable definitions in the model. The usual difficulty is giving the user a convenient means for expressing uncertainty in terms that both the user and the planning sytem understand; a few systems have solved this problem quite successfully.

2. Optimization – The ability to seek the values of a set of the controllable input variables which yield a "best" value of one of the result variables.

The optimization capability is, of course, the subject of the current paper. The general characteristics of this option are described in the next section.

DESIRED CHARACTERISTICS FOR OPTIMIZATION IN PLANNING SYSTEMS

The above described characteristics of both human aided optimization systems and of planning systems suggest several general characteristics which an optimizer in a planning system should contain:

1. It should give the decision maker great flexibility in choosing and changing the parameters of the optimization problem. The chosen model, the measure of performance, the controllable variables, the constraint variables, the ranges of both types of variables, the optimization technique, and the content and format of reports should all be easily settable by the decision maker. The first and last of these capabilities are supplied by the planning system; the balance must come from the optimizer.

2. It should furnish the decision maker intermediate results as they are generated, in the form desired, so that the progress of the optimization can be reviewed as it proceeds.

3. While the decision maker should be able to choose all the parameters of the optimization routine in order to take advantage of whatever problem knowledge there is, default values should be supplied by the system if possible for whatever parameters the decision maker does not wish to specify.

4. Because of the dimensions of the typical problem, the system should have built-in safeguards against large computation time and expense. For example, it should estimate the cost consequences for all but the most trivial search commands and report these to the decision maker before it proceeds with any significant computation requested; it should also provide the option of overriding any such command before it is executed.

5. The system should be interruptable at any point in the analysis with little loss; in particular, the system should always save the best solution obtained to date so that it is not lost when the interrupt option is exercised, and it should permit restarting the solution at that point with no difficulty.

CHARACTERISTICS OF THE IMPLEMENTED SYSTEM

A prototype system which contains all the desirable characteristics described above has been implemented as an experimental option to be used with the EMPIRE planning system. EMPIRE is a proprietary planning system developed by ADR Services, Inc. and supplied by several vendors for both in-house and commercial time-sharing use [1]. It has been used by dozens of companies for analyzing their planning and other management decision problems. It contains all of the modeling, analysis, and report writing options discussed in the above section on planning systems. While EMPIRE was used as the test bed for the prototype optimizer, it is written in FORTRAN and could be used with any planning system containing the basic characteristics discussed above. The interface would be changed to make it compatible with another planning system, but the bulk of the optimization sub-system could be used in its present form.

The hierarchy of the options available in the optimization system is shown in Figure 1. In spite of the nesting, it is quite easy to get from one level to another in order to change any of the optimization characteristics. However, the system insists that previous levels be satisfied before succeeding levels are entered. For example, the objective function must be selected before any decision or constraint variables are specified. As another example, optimization cannot begin until the feasible ranges of the decision variables are meaningful (i.e., the maximum is larger than the minimum).

Three search techniques are available in the implementation, although the modular design allows others to be added as they appear warranted. The three methods currently available include: Search across a regular grid, used when necessary to get the "lay of the land;" random search, used to hunt for as yet undiscovered good combinations of variables and to find a good starting point for hill-climbing; and hill-climbing based on the Rosenbrock method [11], used to fine tune the optimum to the extent desired. The human operator can easily go from one to another of these methods.

The report writing capabilities of EMPIRE are supplemented by the additional reports generated by the optimization system to describe selected variables and their ranges, print intermediate results, and give statistics on searches. Samples of all of these are contained in the Appendix.

The current implementation of the optimization system contains 3-letter mnemonics as command words; less terse commands could easily be implemented if desired. These can be used in several modes, depending on whether the user is specifying or changing a problem, looking at an existing problem, or retrieving a saved problem.

Some default values of the optimization parameters are chosen by the system at the beginning of the optimization session; others are chosen after the objective function, the controllable variables, the constraints and their ranges have been specified by the user, in order to take problem size into account. These parameters include grid size, number of searches, and the other stopping rules associated with the hill-climbing method. Any of these can be changed as desired by the user during the optimization session.

—Choice of performance measure; maximum or minimum

—Choice of controllable and constraint variables

—Ranges of controllable and constraint variables

—Choice of optimization technique

—Optimization parameters

—Execution

HIERARCHY OF OPTIMIZATION OPTIONS

FIGURE 1

EXAMPLE

The planning staff of Advanced Technology Products is using a computer-based planning system to prepare a plan for their newest product line. The marketing research experts believe that base demand BASDEM will be generated by advertising expenditures ADBUD according to the relationship

$$BASDEM = a*ADBUD - b*(ADBUD)**2$$

where the constants a and b are determined by estimating the ADBUD and BASDEM at which saturation of the market takes place. Marketing research also believes that the basic demand can be modified by the selling price PRCBUD, the price influence being representable by

$$ACTDEM = c*BASDEM* (PRCBUD)**(-d)$$

The elasticity d is estimated directly, and c is derived from the nominal price NOMPRC at which ACTDEM = BASDEM. The production department estimates the average direct cost per unit AVGCST by the relationship

$$AVGCST = r + s*exp(-t*ACTDEM)$$

where r and s are obtained from estimates of the average unit cost for one item and infinite items, and t is derived from an estimate of the number of units required to yield an average cost halfway between the two. Finance has determined that the revenue (contribution to overhead and profit) from the product can be computed by

$$REVNUE = ACTDEM (PRCBUD - AVGCST) - ADBUD$$

These features are represented in the EMPIRE model shown in Figure 2. Also contained in the model are the estimated and budgeted data for the product.

The dialog in the Appendix demonstrates the use of the system for solving the planning optimization problem. The base case assumptions are first run without optimization; the expected revenue is found to be $335,130 for ADBUD = $375,000 and PRCBUD = $100. Then the optimization system is entered. The file giving candidate decision and result variables is loaded, and REVNUE is selected as the result to be maximized. Advertising and price are selected as the controllable variables, and ranges are put on both. During this process the system checks that all previous levels in the optimization hierarchy are satisfied.

All three available optimum-seeking methods are used in turn. The default grid search is first run; sixteen trials improve the projected revenue to $353,960 for advertising expenditures of $500,000 and price of $100. A random search is next tried; of the 12 trials, only 1 improves the optimum value. The best revenue found is $354,270 for ADBUD = $503,040 and PRCBUD = $79.42. Finally, the hill-climbing routine is used; after 100 trials the optimal revenue of $358,110 is obtained for ADBUD = $485,220 and PRCBUD = $88.65.

When the optimizing routine is finished, the complete planning report is printed. Management then realizes that the projected demand of 15,730 units exceeds the

```
;ADPOPT. MOD, created 1 Feb 1981 by HURST
;Basic optimization model written in Brussels
option section
      rowtitle 30
      decimal 2
      columnwidth 10
column section
      period "Period"
row section
;input parameters
      SATADE "Saturation ad expend. ($000)" 750
      SATDEM "Saturation demand (U000)" 15
      ELADEM "Demand elasticity (% / / %)" 1.5
      NOMPRC "Nominal selling price ($/ /U)" 100
;controllable variables
      ADBUD "Advertising budget ($000)" 375
      PRCBUD "Budgeted selling price ($/ /U)" 100
;output variables
      BASDEM "Basic demand (U000)"
      ACTDEM "Actual demand (U000)"
      AVGCST "Average unit cost ($/ /U)"
      UNTMRG "Unit margin ($/ /U)"
      SALES "Sales ($000)"
      DIRCST "Direct cost ($000)"
      DIRMRG "Direct margin ($000)"
      REVNUE "Revenue ($000)"
scalar section
;parameters
      CSTONE "One-unit cost ($/ /U)" 45
      CSTINF "Infinite-unit cost ($/ /U)" 30
      NOMUNT "Units for mid-cost (U000)" 10
;intermediate variables
      ADP "Sat. dem./ /Sat. exp. (U/ /$)"
      ARG "Exponent argument ( )"
rules section
      adp=satdem/satade
      basdem=2*adp*adbud-(adp/satade)*adbud*adbud
      actdem=basdem*(nomprc/prcbud)**eladem
      arg=actdem*ln(.5)/nomunt
      avgcst=cstinf+(cstone−cstinf)*expon(arg)
      untmrg=prcbud−avgcst
      sales=actdem*prcbud
      dircst=actdem*avgcst
      dirmrg=sales−dircst
      revnue=dirmrg−adbud
```

EMPIRE MODEL FOR EXAMPLE

FIGURE 2

capacity of the plant, which can make at most 13,000 units. The optimizer is re-entered, ACTDEM is selected as a constraint variable, and an upper limit of 13,000 is imposed. The initial starting point is reset, and the hill-climbing routine is used to determine the new optimal values, which are found to be REVNUE = $354,750 for ADBUD = $470,100 and PRCBUD = $99.55. The complete report shows that the capacity constraint is satisfied for the new values.

OTHER FEATURES OF THE OPTIMIZER

The prototype optimizer has a number of additional features which the simple example did not exploit. Optimization problems and their intermediate solutions can be stored and retrieved from files. During a session, values of all variables can be reset, individually or in groups, to initial, default, or previous values. The user can focus on a region to limit the search of the optimizer. All the tolerances, boundary regions, grid sizes and other parameters of the optimization methods can be changed at any time. Different stopping rules can be activated, including those based on rate of improvement of the solution. All of these other features are designed to give the user better control of the problem and its solution − control which takes advantage of the human's special knowledge about the problem to be solved. That is, after all, the principal advantage HAO has over the more conventional methods of optimization.

BIBLIOGRAPHY

1. Applied Data Research, Inc. *EMPIRE User Reference Manual,* September 1980.

2. Braun, T.H., "The history, evolution, and future of financial planning systems," *ICP Interface,* Spring 1980.

3. Fisher, M.L., Greenfield, A.S., and Jaikumar, R., "A decision support system for vehicle routing," Working Paper HBS 80-62, Division of Research, Graduate School of Business Administration, Harvard University, December 1981.

4. Hamilton, W.F., and Moses, M.A., "An optimization model for corporate financial planning," *Operations Research,* May-June 1973.

5. Hurst, E.G., Jr., "Interactive optimization," Working paper, European Institute for Advanced Studies in Management, October 1972.

6. Hurst, E.G., Jr., "The use of computers in planning," *Encyclopedia of Computer Science,* 2nd edition (to appear).

7. Hurst, E.G., Jr., and Krolak, P.D., "Human aided optimization: An overview," Working Paper 80-08-01, Department of Decision Sciences, The Wharton School, August 1980.

8. Kohner, M.R., "Design and implementation of an interactive optimizer," thesis presented for the degree of Master of Science in Engineering, The Moore School of Electrical Engineering, University of Pennsylvania, August 1981.

9. Krolak, P.D., Felts, W., and Marble, G., "A man-machine approach toward solving the traveling salesman problem," *Communications of the ACM,* Vol 14, 1971.

10. Krolak, P.D., Felts, W., and Nelson, J., "A man-machine approach toward solving various routing, scheduling, and network problems," *Proceedings of the XXL AGARD Meeting (NATO)*, 1971.

11. Rosenbrock, H.H., "An automatic method for finding the greatest or least value of a function," *Computer Journal*, Vol. 3, 1960.

12. Wagner, G.R., "Optimizing decision support systems," *Datamation*, May 1980.

13. Walsh, D.H., and Schechterman, M.D., "Experimental investigation of the usefulness of operator aided optimization in a simulated tactical decision aiding task," Report No. 215-4, Integrated Sciences Corporation, 1978.

APPENDIX

Example of the Dialog with the Optimization Prototype

<u>.RUN ADPOPT</u>　　　　*Begin EMPIRE run.*

```
- - - - - - - - - - - - -
E M P I R E
EXECUTIVE
VER 2A
- - - - - - - - - - - - -
```

YES . . . <u>RUN</u>

"DATA" COMMAND HAS NOT BEEN ISSUED. RESULTS MAY BE INVALID.
ENTER "OK" TO CONTINUE, "RETURN" TO RETURN COMMAND LEVEL:
<u>OK</u>

RUNNING MODEL

Optimize? <u>NO</u>　　　*Run model with input values as base case.*

YES . . . <u>PRINT</u>

ADJUST PAPER, THEN ENTER A CARRIAGE RETURN TO PROCEED=> <u><CR></u>

MODEL:ADPOPT　　　　　DATE: 26-Dec-81　　　12:54　　　PAGE: 1

	Period	
	- - - - - - - - -	
Saturation ad expend. ($000)	750.00	
Saturation demand (U000)	15.00	
Demand elasticity (% / %)	1.50	
Nominal selling price ($/U)	100.00	
Advertising budget ($000)	375.00 ⟵—————	*Controllable*
Budgeted selling price ($/U)	100.00 ⟵—————	*variables*
Basic demand (U000)	11.25	
Actual demand (U000)	11.25	
Average unit cost ($/U)	36.88	
Unit margin ($/U)	63.12	
Sales ($000)	1,125.00	
Direct cost ($000)	414.87	
Direct margin ($000)	710.13	
Revenue ($000)	335.13 ⟵—————	*Result of interest*
One-unit cost ($/U)	45.00	
Infinite-unit cost ($/U)	30.00	
Units for mid-cost (U000)	10.00	
Sat. dem./Sat. exp. (U/$)	.02	
Exponent argument ( )	(.78)	

YES ... <u>RUN</u>

     Optimize? <u>YES</u>   *Begin optimization*

⟫ Entering INTOP optimizer   26–Dec–81   12:55

     Candidate variables' names in default file? ([Y]/N) <u>YES</u>

File "CANDI.DAT " selected for loading

Loading of candidate variables' names completed.
Candidate DeCisions   :   2
Candidate Constraints/Objectives :   8

     Yes? <u>L CDC</u>   *Look at candidate decision variables.*

Candi.DeCis. :	SELec
ADBUD	NO
PRCBUD	NO

     Yes? <u>L CCN</u>   *Look at candidate constraint and objective variables.*

Candid.CoNstr.:	SELec
BASDEM	NO
ACTDEM	NO
AVGCST	NO
UNTMRG	NO
SALES	NO
DIRCST	NO
DIRMRG	NO
REVNUE	NO

     Yes? <u>SDC ADBUD</u>   *Try to select a decision variable ...*

*** No objective & optimization direction selected. *but system wants objective*
                                                            selected first.
.. current dialog LEVel : 1 ("OBJ")

     Yes? <u>MAX REVNUE</u> '   *Objective is to maximize revenue.*

OBJective	:	opt.dir.	[current value	]
REVNUE		MAXimiz.	[0.00	]

     Yes? <u>SDC ADBUD</u>   *Now select ADBUD as decision variable ...*

     Yes? <u>SDC PRCBUD</u> '   *and also PRCBUD (' asks for choice to be echoed).*

Selec. DeCis. :
PRCBUD

     Yes? <u>L CDC</u>   *To verify, look at candidate decision variables.*

Candid.DeCis. :	SELec
ADBUD	YES
PRCBUD	YES

Yes? <u>LAT</u>　　　　　*Try to select the lattice (regular grid) search . . .*

ADBUD	: selected decision whose

ADBUD　　　　　　: selected decision whose
*** lower bound　　=　　　　0.00　not　⟨ higher bound = 　　0.00
PRCBUD　　　　　: selected decision whose
*** lower bound　　=　　　　0.00　not　⟨ higher bound = 　　0.00

. . current dialog LEVel : 3 ("SET")　　*and find that ranges are not yet meaningful.*

Yes? <u>HDC ADBUD 750 '</u>　*Change upper bound of ADBUD . . .*

Selec. DeCis. :　　HIgher Bound
ADBUD　　　　　　　750.00

Yes? <u>RDC PRCBUD 50 125</u>　　*and range of PRCBUD . . .*

Yes? <u>L RDC</u>　　*then look at ranges of decision variables.*

Selec. DeCis. :　　LOwer Bound　　HIgher Bound
ADBUD　　　　　　　0.00　　　　　750.00
PRCBUD　　　　　　50.00　　　　125.00

Yes? <u>LAT '</u>　　*select lattice search technique . . .*

TEChnique selected　:　LATtice search.

Yes? <u>L GRD</u>　　*and look at number of points in the grid . . .*

(LATtice)　　　nb. sampling points in GRiD　　:　　　　16.

Yes? <u>L GAP</u>　　*and at gaps between points.*

Selec. DeCis. :　　sampling GAP
ADBUD　　　　　　　250.00
PRCBUD　　　　　　25.00

Yes? **NEW**   '   *set up a new search.*

OBJective :	opt.dir.	[	current value	]
REVNUE	**MAXimiz.**	[	0.00	]

Nb. of selected decision variables	:	2
Nb. of selected constraint variables	:	0

TEChnique selected : **LATtice** search.

(LATtice)   nb. sampling points in **GRiD** :   16.

OK? ([Y]/N) <u>Y</u>   *Are all the parameters OK?*

Try? <u>Y</u> '   *Try it, and tell us results.*

Grid search completed. :
(LATtice)   nb. sampling points in **GRiD** :   16.

OBJective :	opt.dir.	current value
REVNUE	**MAXimiz.**	353.96

Selec. DeCis. :	LOwer Bound	current VALue	HIgher Bound
ADBUD	0.00	500.00	750.00
PRCBUD	50.00	100.00	125.00

. . no Ignored DeCision.

. . no Selected CoNstraint.

STAtistics:		cumulative	last series
nb. of model runs	:	16	16
nb. of feasible runs	:	16	16
nb. of successful runs	:	6	6
average time per run	:	0.0062 seconds.	

Yes? **RAN** ' *Now select random (Monte Carlo) search technique . . .*

TECHnique selected : RANdom search.

   Yes? **L RUN** *and look at default number of runs.*

(RANdom)   max. nb. model RUNs :   12 [SELECTED],
           currently   :   0

   Yes? **CTN** ' *Set up continuation search.*

OBJective :   opt.dir. [**current value**]
REVNUE   MAXimiz. [**353.96**]

Nb. of selected decision variables   : 2
Nb. of selected constraint variables   : 0

TEChnique selected : RANdom search.

(RANdom)   max. nb. model RUNs :   12 [SELECTED],
           currently   :   0

   OK? ([Y]/N) **Y** *All parameters OK?*

   Try? **Y** ' *Try it, and tell us the results.*

Search stopped upon meeting stopping rule criterion :
(RANdom)   max. nb. models RUNs :   12 [SELECTED],
           currently   :   12 ⟶ binding!

OBJective :   opt.dir.   current value
REVNUE   :   MAXimiz.   354.27

Selec. DeCis. :	LOwer Bound	current VALue	HIgher Bound
ADBUD	0.00	503.04	750.00
PRCBUD	50.00	79.42	125.00

.. no Ignored DeCision.

.. no Selected CoNstraint.

STAtistics:		cumulative	last series
nb. of model runs	:	12	12
nb. of feasible runs	:	12	12
nb. of successful runs	:	1	1
average time per run	:	0.0083 seconds	

Yes? **ROS** '   *Select Rosenbrock (hill climbing) search technique.*

TEChnique selected : ROSenbrock search.

Yes? **L RUN**   *Look at default number of runs . . .*

(ROSenbrock)   **max. nb. model RUNs   :   400 [SELECTED],**
                          currently   :   0

Yes? **RUN 100** *and change it to 100.*

Yes? **INI $ VAL** ' *Initialize search at best point found to date.*

Selec. DeCis. :   INItial value
ADBUD   503.04
PRCBUD   79.42

        Yes? NEW '   *Set up new search.*

OBJective   :   opt.dir.   [current value   ]
REVNUE   MAXimiz.   [354.27   ]

Nb. of selected decision variables   :   2
Nb. of selected constraint variables :   0

TEChnique selected : ROSenbrock search.

(ROSenbrock)   max. nb. model RUNs   :   100 [SELECTED],
                      currently   :   0

BOUndary region relative width   : 0.1000E−02 [SELECTED].

        OK? ([Y]/N) Y   *Everything OK?*

        Try? LIM 10 R '   *Do 10 runs, give us the intermediate results.*

. . Optimum search interrupted upon request
     after   10 model runs.

OBJective   :   opt.dir.   current value
REVNUE   MAXimiz.   358.08

Selec. DeCis. :   LOwer Bound   current VALue   HIgher Bound
ADBUD   0.00   488.04   750.00
PRCBUD   50.00   89.17   125.00

. . no Selected CoNstraint.

STAtistics: cumulative   last series
        nb. of model runs   :   10   10
        nb. of feasible runs :   10   10
        nb. of successful runs :   6   6
        average time per run :   0.0100 seconds.

        Try? Y '   *Finish the 100 runs.*

Search stopped upon meeting stopping rule criterion :
(ROSenbrock)   max. nb. model RUNs   :   100 [SELECTED],
                      currently   :   100 −−−➤ binding!

OBJective   :   opt.dir.   current value
REVNUE   MAXimiz.   358.11

Selec. DeCis. :   LOwer Bound   current VALue   HIgher Bound
ADBUD   0.00   485.22   750.00
PRCBUD   50.00   88.65   125.00

. . no Ignored DeCision.

. . no Selected CoNstraint.

STAtistics: cumulative   last series
        nb. of model runs   :   100   90
        nb. of feasible runs :   100   90
        nb. of successful runs :   18   12
        average time per run :   0.0030 seconds

Yes? **EOS**   *Leave optimizer.*

Leaving INTOP optimizer   26—Dec—81   13:07

YES . . . **PRINT**

ADJUST PAPER, THEN ENTER A CARRIAGE RETURN TO PROCEED=> <CR>

MODEL:ADPOPT   DATE: 26—Dec—81   13:07   PAGE: 1

	Period	
Saturation ad expend. ($000)	750.00	
Saturation demand (U000)	15.00	
Demand elasticity (%/%)	1.50	
Nominal selling price ($/U)	100.00	
Advertising budget ($000)	485.22	◄—————— *Controllable variable*
Budgeted selling price ($/U)	88.65	◄—————— *values . . .*
Basic demand (U000)	13.13	
Actual demand (U000)	15.73	
Average unit cost ($/U)	35.04	
Unit margin ($/U)	53.61	
Sales ($000)	1,394.60	
Direct cost ($000)	551.27	
Direct margin ($000)	843.33	
Revenue ($000)	358.11	◄—————— *which lead to the maxi-*
One-unit cost ($/U)	45.00	*mum value of revenue.*
Infinite-unit cost ($/U)	30.00	
Units for mid-cost (U000)	10.00	
Sat. dem./Sat. exp. (U/$)	.02	
Exponent argument ( )	(1.09)	

YES . . . **RUN**

Optimize? **Y**

>>> Entering INTOP optimizer   26—Dec—81   13:08

Yes? **SCN ACTDEM**   *Select ACTDEM as a constraint variable . . .*

Yes? **HCN ACTDEM 13**   *set an upper limit of 13 . . .*

Yes? **L RCN**   *and look at the ranges of the constraint variables.*

Selec. CoNstr.:	LOwer Bound	HIgher Bound
ACTDEM	0.00	**13.00**

Yes? **INI $ MOI '**   *set controllable variables to their model input (base case)*
                    values.

Selec. DeCis. :	INitial value
ADBUD	375.00
PRCBUD	100.00

Yes? <u>NEW</u>   *Set up new search . . .*

Try? <u>LIM 10 R</u> '   *and give us intermediate results after 10 runs.*

.. Optimum search interrupted upon request
    after   10 model runs.

OBJective	:	opt.dir.	current value	
REVNUE		MAXimiz.	346.10	

Selec. DeCis. :	LOwer Bound	current VALue	HIgher Bound
ADBUD	0.00	405.00	750.00
PRCBUD	50.00	95.13	125.00

Selec. CoNstr. :	LOwer Bound	current VALue	HIgher Bound
ACTDEM	0.00	12.75	13.00

STAtistics:	cumulative	last series
nb. of model runs :	10	10
nb. of feasible runs :	8	8
nb. of successful runs :	6	6
average time per run :	0.0000 seconds	

Try? <u>Y</u> '   *Finish the search.*

Search stopped upon meeting stopping rule criterion :
(ROSenbrock)   max. nb. model RUNs   :   100 [SELECTED],
    currently   :   100 ——➤ binding!

OBJective	:	opt.dir.	current value	
REVNUE		MAXimiz.	354.72	

Selec. DeCis. :	LOwer Bound	current VALue	HIgher Bound
	0.00	469.21	750.00
	50.00	99.52	125.00

.. no Ignored DeCision.

Selec. CoNstr. :	LOwer Bound	current VALue	HIgher Bound
	0.00	12.99	13.00

STAtistics:	cumulative	last series
nb. of model runs :	100	90
nb. of feasible runs :	80	72
nb. of successful runs :	35	29
average time per run :	0.0020 seconds	

Yes? **L BOU**   *Look at the boundary condition . . .*

BOUndary region relative width   :   0.1000E−02 [SELECTED].

Yes? **BOU .00001 '**   *and narrow it.*

BOUndary region relative width   :   0.1000E−04 [SELECTED].

Yes? **CTN '**   *Set up a continuation search.*

OBJective   :   opt.dir.   [current value   ]
REVnue   MAXimiz.   [354.72   ]

Nb. of selected decision variables   :   2
Nb. of selected constraint variables :   1

TEChnique selected   : ROSenbrock search.

(ROSenbrock)   max. nb. model RUNs   :   100 [SELECTED],
                        currently   :   0

BOUndary region relative width   : 0.1000E−04

OK? ([Y]/N) Y   *Everything OK?*

Try? **LIM 10 R '**   *Give us results after 10 runs.*

.. Optimum search interrupted upon request
      after   10 model runs.

OBJective   :   opt.dir.   current value
REVNUE   MAXimiz.   354.75

Selec. DeCis. :   LOwer Bound   current VALue   HIgher Bound
ADBUD   0.00   470.10   750.00
PRCBUD   50.00   99.55   125.00

Selec. CoNstr. :   LOwer Bound   current VALue   HIgher Bound
                       0.00   13.00   13.00

STAtistics: cumulative   last series
      nb. of model runs   :   10   10
      nb. of feasible runs   :   8   8
      nb. of successful runs :   5   5
      average time per run   :   0.0000 seconds

<u>Try? Y</u> '   *Finish the search.*

Search stopped upon meeting stopping rule criterion :

(ROSenbrock)	max. nb. model RUNs	:	100 [SELECTED],
	currently	:	100 − − ⇒ binding!

OBJective	:	opt.dir.	current value
REVNUE		MAXimiz.	354.75

Selec. DeCis. :	LOwer Bound	current VALue	HIgher Bound
ADBUD	0.00	470.19	750.00
PRCBUD	50.00	99.55	125.00

.. no Ignored DeCision.

Selec. CoNstr. :	LOwer Bound	current VALue	HIgher Bound
	0.00	13.00	13.00

STAtistics:	cumulative	last series
nb. of model runs :	100	90
nb. of feasible runs :	77	69
nb. of successful runs :	23	18
average time per run :	0.0030 seconds	

Yes? <u>EOS</u>   *Leave optimizer*

Leaving INTOP optimizer   26–Dec–81   13:16

YES . . . <u>PRINT</u>

ADJUST PAPER, THEN ENTER A CARRIAGE RETURN TO PROCEED=> <u><CR></u>

MODEL:ADPOPT   DATE: 26–Dec–81   13:16   PAGE: 1

	Period
	- - - - - - - -
Saturation ad expend. ($000)	750.00
Saturation demand (U000)	15.00
Demand elasticity (%/%)	1.50
Nominal selling price ($/U)	100.00
Advertising budget ($000)	470.19 ←
Budgeted selling price ($/U)	99.55 ←
Basic demand (U000)	12.91
Actual demand (U000)	13.00 ←
Average unit cost ($/U)	36.09
Unit margin ($/U)	63.46
Sales ($000)	1,294.14
Direct cost ($000)	469.19
Direct margin ($000)	824.95
Revenue ($000)	354.75 ←
One-unit cost ($/U)	45.00
Infinite-unit cost ($/U)	30.00
Units for mid-cost (U000)	10.00
Sat. dem./Sat. exp. (U/$)	.02
Exponent argument ( )	(.90)

Values of controllable variables . . .

which satisfy the constraint . . .

and maximize revenue while doing so.

YES . . . <u>EXIT</u>

E M P I R E — END OF SESSION

DECISION SUPPORT SYSTEMS
M.J. Ginzberg, W. Reitman, E.A. Stohr (editors)
North-Holland Publishing Company
© DSS, 1982

DECISION SUPPORT MODELS FOR FLEET PLANNING
by
M. Edelstein and M. Melnyk
The Hertz Corporation

INTRODUCTION

The car rental business has grown and changed dramatically. Unprecedented demand for rental vehicles, a growing number of companies, and intense price competition have transformed this industry into an integral part of the total transportation system in the U.S. Throughout this period, Hertz has maintained and enhanced its position in the market place.

There are many reasons for this success. Foremost among them is Hertz management's ability to plan for and respond to ever-changing conditions. Specifically, Hertz management can continuously assess and evaluate fleet requirements versus anticipated demand. Quick response is essential in maintaining the critical balance between supply and demand in the car rental business. Both supply and demand are complex variables, with long term and short term dimensions.

Demand depends on overall industry growth, pricing, promotional policies, and competitive conditions. In determining demand, Hertz relies on local assessment of the marketplace. Once the demand assessment has been made, supply is treated as a control variable. Relative to a given demand level, there is an appropriate number of cars needed to satisfy the customer with a high level of service. Because of lead-time and logistical considerations, the process of guaranteeing proper overall supply starts months in advance. Once the correct fleet level is achieved in an area, the next step is to determine appropriate distribution strategies on a day-to-day basis. Finally, local management fine-tunes supply on an hour-by-hour basis during the day.

Much of Hertz's success in addressing the supply problem is due to management tools developed by the Hertz Operations Research Group. These tools are interactive, computer-based models which have been developed jointly with management to address each of the three parts of the fleet planning process — long-term, short-term, and immediate.

The tools described in this paper deal directly with the heart of the car rental business. Vehicles are installed and deleted from the fleet, available inventory is distributed daily from city to city, and business levels are monitored and controlled hour by hour, all with the assistance of these time-share-based simulations models. Because the manager relies on these systems so intensely, the approach used is a descriptive rather than a prescriptive one. The field manager with profit responsibility is not likely to surrender that responsibility to a complex computer model which he does not understand.

From the outset, field input was critical to the development effort. The critical elements of the fleet planning and management process were extracted and put together in a comprehensive and consistent manner, with the computer serving as a powerful computational aid. The tools were developed to more fully utilize the

The Hertz RAC Field Organization chart is shown below:

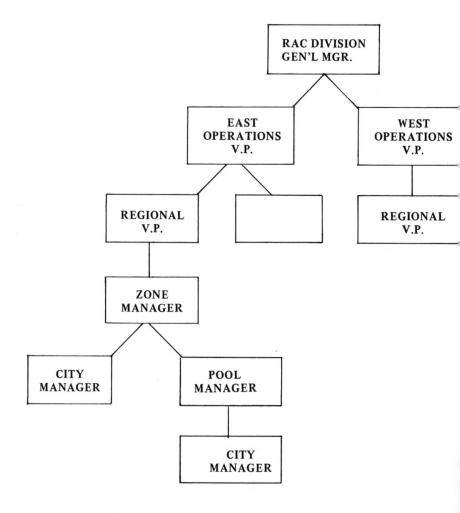

FIGURE 1.

The organization is set up geographically with 8 to 15 cities comprising a zone and 2 to 4 zones in a region.

This chart indicates the hierarchical nature of the review process. Computer terminals are located in managers' offices at each level of the organization. This computer-based communications network is bi-directional and has proven to be indispensable to the decision making, review, and control process.

manager's judgement, experience and insight, not to replace them.

In using these systems, the manager typically takes the best information available at the time, specifies his assumptions, incorporates his judgement, and then runs the model. An instantaneous evaluation based on these inputs is then produced. The manager is liberated to think creatively and experiment with various strategies by changing the input to the model. He normally runs the model iteratively to arrive at a final strategy. In this manner, the model is part of the decision-making process and the manager relates to it as his tool for better decision-making.

THE LONG-TERM PROBLEM — FLEET PLANNING

The Problem.

Planning for an adequate fleet is a complex process — the proper level and mix must be considered. The proper level depends on local demand, which fluctuates from month to month. The strategy is: fleet up to coincide with the forecasted peaks and valleys which result from seasonality, special events and overall business growth. Too many cars incur unnecessary expense. Too few cars mean lost opportunity and profit. How should deliveries and disposals be timed to achieve a maximum fit with the expected demand pattern?

Hertz has several ways to increase its fleet: purchase, lease, purchase with a buy-back arrangement, or transfer from another location. When disposal is necessary, Hertz can sell its cars retail or wholesale, transfer them to another location, or turn them back to the lessee or dealer. Each of these methods has its benefits and draw-backs. The typical fleet supply strategy will use several of these combinations each month. Finally, these more general timing and method considerations must be translated to specific models of cars.

The Process.

The fleet planning model is an analytical tool that helps management develop a vehicle installation and disposal schedule, and it instantaneously evaluates the adequacy of the resulting fleet level. This model is illustrated in Figure 2. A set of equations establishes the relationships between the fleet- and rental-related variables for each month in the planning horizon. The model then generates the necessary financial and operational statistics which measure the viability of a proposed plan.

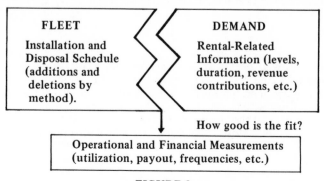

FIGURE 2

For example, a simulated upward change in a demand variable will result in more revenue and greater use of a given fleet level. This may or may not be feasible. Increasing the fleet in a given month may solve a current shortage but create a surplus fleet problem in later months.

Hertz may or may not offset this surplus by selling or otherwise disposing of cars, depending on market conditions. The model readily evaluates these strategies and tradeoffs. A whole series of alternatives can be developed quickly and easily because this is done interactively by computer.

The system greatly facilitates the management review process since standardized pro forma documents are produced by the model and are accessible to all levels of management. Suggestions and criticisms are analyzed using the computer. In this mode, the interactive system can process and evaluate management judgements and ideas. As a result, the focus of the planning and review process is on strategy, not on the large number of computations that must routinely be performed to develop a coherent plan for the future.

The Data Base.

The data used and generated by the model is stored in a data base. Managers can retrieve this information and design reports to meet their specific needs. Senior management can focus on the overall direction of the business by running a division-level report over a specific time frame. Zone managers can rank their cities by a specific criterion to highlight relative performance. Reports can be generated based on actual performance: these highlight trends and identify problem areas.

In addition, a complete description of the current fleet is available for instant retrieval and analysis to assist in the planning process. For example, fleet-age information can be generated to forecast profit and loss for planned car sales. Inventory reports for specific model cars can be produced to spot imbalances in model and size mix. The instantaneous accessibility to critical current and past information provides a strong foundation for the formulation of strategies.

**THE SHORT-TERM PROBLEM –
DAILY PLANNING AND DISTRIBUTION.**

Once the fleet level is determined and fixed in a given time frame, the operational problem of managing the fleet on a day-to-day basis remains.

The Problem.

The field operations are set up either as "independent cities" or as "pools." An independent city owns its fleet of vehicles, and all fleet-related decisions are made by local management. In a pool, the fleet is shared by a group of cities. Each city is run by its own management, but fleet administration is centralized. Distribution and control of the fleet rest with the distribution manager. The distribution manager works closely with each of the cities and the zone manager, who has overall operating responsibility for the pool. Most of the major Hertz field operations are organized as pools consisting of from 2 to 15 cities with fleets of 2,000 to 15,000 cars. The potential for improving fleet use is a major benefit of this setup since shortages in one city can be filled with another city's slack.

The distribution process basically consists of three steps as depicted in Figure 3. The first step is a demand potential and capacity assessment. Before any distribution decision can be made, two critical numbers for each city for each day in the planning horizon must be determined: the number of customers potentially available to Hertz (the demand potential) and the number of cars available for rental (the rental capacity).

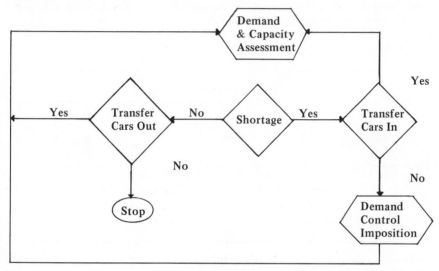

FIGURE 3

The second step is to determine a distribution strategy. The rental capacity estimate is compared to the estimated demand potential in each city to determine which cities have shortages and which have excesses. Appropriate vehicle transfers are then proposed.

The last step is a demand control imposition. If it is concluded that shortages will still remain in some cities, then a recommendation to control demand in these cities is made to the zone manager. Demand can be restricted by limiting reservations and/or renting only to customers with reservations.

The most critical determination of all, available capacity, is highly complex and uncertain. New cars are always being installed and other cars being retired. Cars are continuously going in and coming out of shops or being moved from city to city. But more importantly, at any given time, the available fleet is being depleted by new rentals and replenished by vehicles returned from previous rentals. In addition, because of the Hertz "Rent-It-Here, Leave-It-There" policy, current and future rentals can occur anywhere and return anywhere. Therefore, both the impact of distribution-imposed intercity vehicle transfers and the results of customer flow between pool cities must be directly accounted for.

The problem, then, is to accurately forecast the future demand and the fleet availability for each city during each day in the planning horizon. In addition, based on this determination, various transfer or demand control policies must be assessed.

The Process.

Figure 4 describes the system flow. Daily, each city manager completes a form that includes actual data from the prior day and projections for future days for his city. This data is telecopied to the distribution manager. He, in turn, inputs this data and some of his own into the daily planning and distribution aid (DPDA) via a timesharing terminal. This data is fed to the model — a set of recursive sequential equations describing the timing of rentals, check ins and flow between cities.

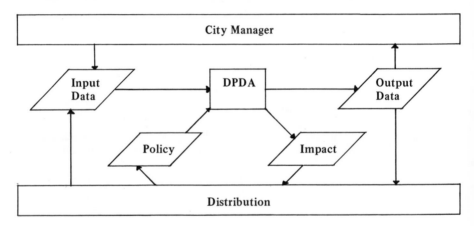

FIGURE 4

The model produces a report forecasting the situation in each city for the coming week. This report lets management distribute the fleet based on the predictions. A sample report is shown in Figure 5. In this illustration, city A has anticipated shortages during the middle of the week and on the weekend. City B has shortages predicted for the end of the week. City C seems to have excess cars throughout the week.

Based on these projections some transfer of cars, from B and/or C to A, seems logical. The question is: how many and when? For example, moving too many cars from B to A on Monday may move up the shortage in city B from Saturday to Wednesday or Thursday, with no cars available to alleviate the problem. The net result would only be to transfer the shortage and incur car transfer expenses. On the other hand, some movement is clearly justified due to the projected surplus at B and C for the next few days. The model, because it accounts for the timing of rentals, check ins, and customer flow between city locations, can quickly simulate the impact of any transfer and/or demand control policy and help establish the most balanced solution.

CITY A	MON	TUE	WED	THR	FRI	SAT	SUN
IDLE	527	82	0	0	14	167	0
CHECK-INS	285	410	518	571	743	274	419
INTERCITY TRANSFERS	0	0	0	0	0	0	0
AVAILABLE FLEET	832	492	518	571	767	446	419
DEMAND PROJECTION	750	700	605	557	600	490	600
CARS LEFT OVER	82	-208	-87	14	167	-44	-188

CITY B							
IDLE	80	162	149	122	86	5ì	0
CHECK-INS	196	106	92	126	195	107	125
INTERCITY TRANSFERS	0	0	0	0	0	0	0
AVAILABLE FLEET	272	264	237	244	296	159	123
DEMAND PROJECTION	110	115	115	158	245	163	119
CARS LEFT OVER	162	149	122	86	51	-4	4

CITY C							
IDLE	80	57	47	31	51	74	71
CHECK-INS	118	112	100	120	141	97	73
INTERCITY TRANSFERS	0	0	0	0	0	0	0
AVAILABLE FLEET	192	167	141	146	189	156	140
DEMAND PROJECTION	135	120	110	95	115	85	80
CARS LEFT OVER	57	47	31	51	74	71	60

FIGURE 5

Figure 6 illustrates the final strategy to use the fleet effectively while guaranteeing a high level of service. Note that a substantial number of cars is moved into A from B and C. In spite of this, demand control is needed to keep fleet supply and rental demand in balance. Demand for Tuesday in city A is reduced by 100.

The Data Base.

A data base develops as a by-product of runs using the model. This lets management study in detail the car rental business patterns in any city for any time period. For example, suppose that a proposal to charge the customer for not returning the car to the renting city (a drop-off charge) is being considered. The system provides a detailed check-in analysis indicating the degree of current customer movement between pool cities. This information is useful in determing when and where the charge should apply. After the drop-off charge policy has been established, the report is used to monitor the policy's impact.

As another example, consider a situation in which the average revenue per rental has declined suddenly for the pool. A rental length analysis report displays length-of-rental statistics for each of the pool cities during the recent period and shows if length of rental or some other factor is responsible.

THE IMMEDIATE PROBLEM –
HOURLY AVAILABILITY

Once a transfer and/or control policy has been determined, the focus is on getting through the current day, guaranteeing immediate vehicle availability for arriving Hertz customers.

The Problem.

The DPDA provides a picture of total fleet availability versus demand for a given day. Both of these may have been adjusted as needed to guarantee a car for each expected customer. This overall adjustment now needs to be refined. For example, a contemplated demand control measure at a major airport (limiting reservations, or renting only to customers with reservations) may need to be concentrated in the morning hours when most of the day's rentals take place.

The amount of demand control needed, and for which hours, depends upon the specific hourly rental patterns. In addition, the number and distribution of check ins for that day needs to be considered since check ins replenish the available fleet. Finally, other factors affect fleet availability – the number of cars returning from shop maintenance, being newly delivered, or leaving the fleet must be evaluated. Without considering these factors, too much business might possibly be turned away. On the other hand, not enough demand control may result in dissatisfied customers who arrive to find no car waiting for them.

The Process.

Several times each day, the manager enters data on the current status of his business – the number of available cars, and a forecast of rentals and check ins for the remainder of the day.

CITY A	MON	TUE	WED	THR	FRI	SAT	SUN
IDLE	527	173	54	52	120	291	91
CHECK-INS	286	432	572	625	761	284	436
INTERCITY TRANSFERS	90	50	0	0	0	0	0
AVAILABLE FLEET	923	654	627	677	891	581	527
DEMAND PROJECTION	750	600	575	557	600	490	500
CARS LEFT OVER	173	54	52	120	291	91	27

CITY B							
IDLE	80	97	35	22	29	18	11
CHECK-INS	196	107	91	111	164	86	91
INTERCITY TRANSFERS	-65	-50	0	0	0	0	0
AVAILABLE FLEET	207	150	122	129	208	106	101
DEMAND PROJECTION	110	115	100	100	190	95	90
CARS LEFT OVER	97	35	22	29	18	11	11

CITY C							
IDLE	80	32	23	16	37	57	50
CHECK-INS	118	113	99	121	138	93	71
INTERCITY TRANSFERS	-25	0	0	0	0	0	0
AVAILABLE FLEET	167	143	116	132	172	135	118
DEMAND PROJECTION	135	120	100	95	115	80	80
CARS LEFT OVER	32	23	16	37	57	50	38

FIGURE 6

The model uses this input as well as the relative pattern based on rental and check-in flow histories to determine fleet availability hour-by-hour. A sample report is shown in Figure 7. Note that this report predicted no cars left for rental during the noon hours. This advance notice of an expected shortage allowed local management to remedy the situation by augmenting the fleet with transfer, accelerated repair work in the shop and other supply tactics. As a demand tactic, they could impose appropriate demand control measures. The model quickly evaluated any proposed measures and in an interactive fashion led the manager to the proper mix of available alternatives to develop a final strategy.

The Data Base.

The data base created by the system allows analysis of customer rental and check-in patterns. This information has been used for a variety of purposes. For example, staff scheduling at the rental counters has to match the frequency of customer arrivals. Similarly, the scheduling of garagemen who clean and wash returning cars and do routine maintenance depends on the flow of returning renters and arriving customers. Enough returning cars have to be "processed" to satisfy arriving renters. Thus, proper garagemen staffing depends directly on the rates of check-ins versus rentals. A separate subsystem for this purpose has been developed and used with success.

PERSPECTIVE

All fleet related decisions throughout the country are made with these systems. Fleet plans generated by the fleet planning model are the basis for generating orders and disposal plans for vehicles. These plans are reviewed several times a month, with a planning horizon for 1 year for each city in the country. As business conditions and management strategy evolve, plans are revised and results are continuously evaluated, The system has the flexibility to focus on geographic regions and diversified markets. In this way, emerging trends can be discussed and the fleet can be adjusted to meet the situations. Another important feature of the FPM is that senior management can "pull up" the latest fleet plan for any city in the country at any time and at any location. This communications flexibility stimulates analysis and invariably leads to better fleet planning.

The Daily Planning and Distribution Aid is the tool used to properly distribute cars to meet expected business levels. It has been used successfully to manage such events as the Olympics, the Super Bowl, the Florida Christmas season and business conventions. Each of these events involves unusual rental patterns and tremendous business volatility. If a competitor runs out of cars, or stops taking reservations, the impact on Hertz's business can be quite significant. The model successfully simulates the effect of these emerging conditions. The flexibility and user orientation of these tools has made them indispensable to the field in achieving good utilization with excellent customer service.

The success of these models demonstrates how system technology can be creatively applied to a complex business environment. The keys to success are field involvement from the outset, user-oriented system design, and progressive management support.

	HOURS	START	CHECK-INS	ADJUST	AVAIL-FLEET	RENTALS	CARS LEFT
AM	7:00—8:00	180	20	0	200	43	156
	8:00—9:00	156	17	0	173	53	120
	9:00—10:00	120	17	26	163	63	101
	10:00—11:00	191	15	0	116	64	51
	11:00—12:00	51	17	-5	63	84	-20
PM	12:00—1:00	0	20	0	20	82	-62
	1:00—2:00	0	27	-20	7	19	-12
	2:00—3:00	0	37	0	37	5	32
	3:00—4:00	32	54	30	116	8	108
	4:00—5:00	108	61	0	169	50	119
	5:00—6:00	119	42	0	161	21	140
	6:00—7:00	140	32	0	174	13	161
	7:00—8:00	161	15	0	176	40	136
	8:00—9:00	136	10	0	146	18	128
	9:00—10:00	128	10	0	138	18	120
	10:00—11:00	120	2	0	123	5	118
	11:00—12:00	118	2	0	120	6	114

FIGURE 7

DECISION SUPPORT SYSTEMS
M.J. Ginzberg, W. Reitman, E.A. Stohr (editors)
North-Holland Publishing Company
© DSS, 1982

DESIGNING A DECISION SUPPORT SYSTEM FOR A
CHANGING BELL SYSTEM
by
John W. Jeske, Jr.
American Telephone and Telegraph Company

I. INTRODUCTION

Looking ahead to the possibility that parts of the Bell System business may be detariffed, and anticipating some restructuring, it has become apparent that there will be a need for major shifts in the decision making process of the corporation. It is believed that this will require the design and implementation of the most effective decision support system possible, and practical. Even without possible restructuring, decision support systems are under continuous review and improvement.

The purpose of this paper is to provide some insight into the technical aspects of the processes being utilized as well as what the decision support system may look like in a restructured Bell System. Particular emphasis will be given to the capital budgeting and resource allocation problems, with sufficient background to clarify the interrelationship of financial and strategic planning with the resources allocation process. Particularly, this paper will deal with technical decisions regarding the evolution of a new decision support system, some insight on the problems of accomplishing its development and implementation, and a description of a proposed system.

It is important to emphasize that the ultimate system will, in reality, evolve from the interactions of many functional executives and managers. This paper is an early view by a management science manager, who, while having significant responsibilities in the implementation of the ultimate architecture, will be directed by the functional executives and managers as to what will be the actual decision process.

II. THE FACTORS OF CHANGE

Since the Bell System has been, for a very long period of time, a large and successful corporation, it may seem strange to hear someone state that it is in the process of designing a new decision support system. The reason why a new decision support system is necessary is that the very nature of the business of the Bell System is undergoing radical changes. There are a variety of reasons, both internal and external, that are causing these changes. Knowledge of the factors which are driving these changes will enable one to more fully understand the logic for, and the design of, the new decision support system.

There are many factors that are causing the Bell System to change. While most of these are interrelated, I will attempt to individually discuss them to give you some idea of their impact.

Perhaps the primary driving force behind this change is technology. Technological change can be separated into two types. One affects the supply side of the business and the other the demand side. The supply side has to do with the evolution of chips, computers, satellites, optical fibers, and other high-technology items. What this means is that there is a rapid evolution of new products coming into the market that can either do new things or do old things better and always at a lower cost. It would not be as important a factor if there were not equally dramatic changes on the demand side. Many of you may be familiar with the term "The Information Handling and Management Market." In our complex society the value of information, and the necessity of manipulating and using that information, has become a critical factor in our economy.

Another exogenous factor that is causing change in our business is the major shift in government's attitude toward regulation. For Bell, it would be more correct to call it the evolution of a detariffed environment. We have such examples as the airline and securities industries in which deregulation has already taken place. Also the leadership of the current federal government appears to have a mandate from the electorate for further deregulation. A start has already occurred in the telecommunications industry with the Federal Communications Commission (FCC) rulings in what is referred to as "Computer Inquiry II" (F.C.C. Docket No. 20828). These rulings grew out of an FCC attempt to decide what should be the boundaries of the regulated telecommunications industry in relation to those of the computer industry.

The bottom line of the inquiry was that there is no logical definitional separation; they are one — both are in the Information Market. The result of those hearings was an order that permitted the Bell System to participate in a significant manner on a detariffed basis in the provision of enhanced services which were defined as the combination of basic transmission service with computer processing applications which serve to act on the form, control, code, protocol, or similar aspects of the subscribers' transmitted information; to provide the subscriber additional, different or restructured information or which involves subscriber interaction with stored information; in the provision of technologically advanced communications processing; as well as to continue in its current customer premises equipment line of business. However, certain limitations were placed on that participation. The principal limitation is the requirement to set up a fully separated subsidiary or subsidiaries to minimize the possibility that there could be any cost cross-subsidization between the regulated business and the detariffed businesses.

A third factor that is causing changes in the business and the way it is operated are current and long term economic expectations. We now have double digit inflation, and former expectations that it would run at about 3 or 4 percent per year have dramatically changed. The most optimistic long run estimates include numbers greater than 8 percent. This situation has rendered obsolete many of the financial arrangements that are in place for providing telecommunications service. An example of this is the capitalization of station connection charges.

Another economic factor is the cost, and availability, of energy. It has been determined to be a limited and expensive resource. Because it is now being priced much closer to its true economic cost, obvious cross-elasticities are being recognized, including those with communications and information management. Another economic condition that has an impact on the way businesses can operate, including the Bell System, is the greater prominence of the international market and foreigh competition. It is recognized that most domestic corporations have to be allowed to fully compete in the international market.

Coupled with the above realities of technology, regulatory environment, and eco-

THE PRESENT BELL SYSTEM

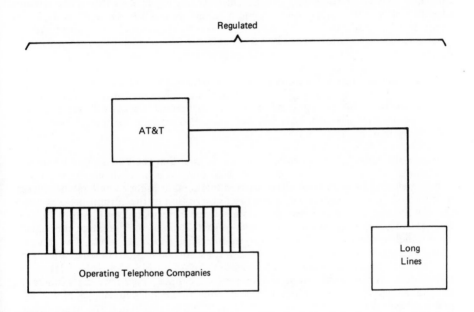

Figure 1

nomic conditions, are three legal events. One is known as the Consent Decree of 1956. That decree was the result of the settlement of a prior antitrust suit brought against the Bell System by the Department of Justice (DOJ). It contains a major limitation generally restricting the Bell System to the regulated telecommunications market. Currently, there is another DOJ—AT&T antitrust suit which is an attempt to restructure the Bell System. Finally, in the congress, legislation is now being developed to revamp the Communications Act of 1934. This legislation, if passed, should provide much needed clarification of the Bell System in the Communications Information Industry.

While some changes will be mandated, and some will be self-initiated, the management of the Bell System at AT&T is proceeding with planning for the restructuring of the business based on its best guess as to what the various changes will require. The impact of these changes will be significant enough to result in a major restructuring of the Bell System.

The basic thrust in the above activities is to direct that the Bell System become a less integrated business and have entities which operate as independent businesses in both detariffed regulated and unregulated markets. In order to understand the significance of these changes, I will give a brief description of the current organization of the Bell System, whose business is now almost totally regulated. In Figure 1 the central control point of the business is labeled AT&T. Each of the operating companies has a franchise to provide telephone service to certain geographic areas. The services provided include equipment, local service, intra-state connections between local services and other related services. To the right of the AT&T block, is a block labeled Long Lines. This organization provides inter-state connections between the operating telephone companies. Long Lines also interconnects the independent telephone companies. What is important in regard to a decision support system, is the relationship between AT&T and its operating units. Each company independently develops what is called a construction program, which is its need for capital in the current year. In addition, AT&T maintains a continuous review of the operating plans of the Bell Telephone companies. For example, each telephone company has a network engineering organization. There is also a network engineering organization at AT&T. Finally, Western Electric has the production facilities that make the network equipment and Bell Telephone Laboratories has the capability to do the research and development. Through the close coordination of the research, development, manufacturing, and operating units, the network function is designed, controlled, and operated in a closed loop fashion by headquarter/subordinate organizations. This would be true of other functions such as local service, terminal equipment and of others that might be referred to as product lines of the Bell System. The method of assembling construction programs is a bottom-up analysis, based on engineering economics, of the best way to perform the function, coupled with the franchise requirement that the Bell System must provide all the services reasonably required. While there are areas of flexibility in putting together a construction program, basically such a program is demand-driven, and the areas in which the businesses operate are rigorously defined. The fiscal control is really based on the integration of the functions.

As previously discussed, the general tenor of the regulatory and legislative activities indicates the potential for some basic restructuring of the business. In Figure 2 the central control unit is now labeled, Parent Company. It is my view that such a Parent Company will operate more as a portfolio management and capital generation

THE FUTURE BELL SYSTEM?

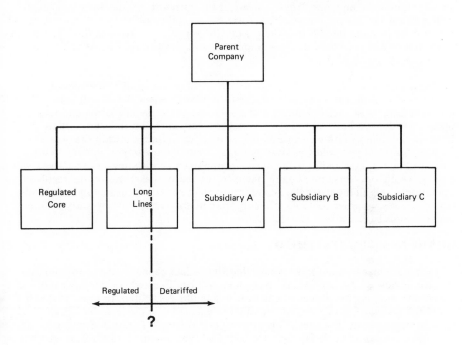

Figure 2

unit, rather than as a functional control unit as was previously described. This doesn't imply that, where legally permissible, the parent company will not remain operations oriented. In addition, some lines of business will be split into either regulated detariffed or unregulated businesses. These are represented by the boxes labeled "Subsidiary A, B, and C." On the extreme left of the control line below Parent Company are the regulated companies. These consist of the current operating telephone companies minus the lines of business that form the separate entities to the right. A caveat which must be mentioned is that the organization plan is in a state of flux. The above is illustrative and presented in order to provide a framework for discussing the decision support system problems.

The organization shown in Figure 2 makes apparent that a different method for resource allocation will be required in the future Bell System. There will have to be a different kind of financial planning and assurance so that the allocation and financial planning is done in best interests of the stakeholders of the business because there will be more flexibility (with a corresponding chance for optimization) in the separated entities. Strategic and policy analysis will play a much more important role. While there will be this new and dynamic business opportunity with new entities, there will still be the historic corporate commitment to the traditional service in the regulated operations. This all indicates the need for a strong financial focus in corporate decision processes. In order to do its job, corporate management will obviously need new support tools to effectively play its role.

III. THE PROBLEM STATEMENT

Corporate management must insure that the various capital budget proposals are studied in view of a variety of criteria (which will be discussed later in this paper) to determine what capital is needed and how it should be allocated. In order to understand the extent of change engendered by the planned new process, the current decision process must be discussed. This process(1) is shown in Figure 3. Starting at the top, there is a round circle labeled "Customers." In economic terms, this is where the demand is created. Starting with demand, which drives the process, customers use a service generating a flow labeled "S Revenues."

From this stream of funds, depreciation and earnings available for reinvesting are outputs. Based on plant and working capital changes dictated by the service demands of the customers (we have closed the loop), additional capital from the equity and debt markets (and lessors) is produced to fill in those capital requirements not satisfied by the internally generated funds. As has been mentioned, this entire process is demand driven and restricted to the narrow range of traditional telecommunications services. The basis for determining the means of provision of each service demand is by the use of engineering economic studies and long-term technological programs. Historically, this provided a very efficient way of running the business. However, with the establishment of additional separate entities, and the possibility that the Parent will have to deal at "arms length" with some of them, an entirely different decision support system is indicated.

In order to prepare for what is needed in the future, corporate management must insure that standards are provided to Bell entities for project evaluation including such elements as input guidelines, forecasting specifications, standard analytics and basic outputs.

THE FINANCIAL PROCESS

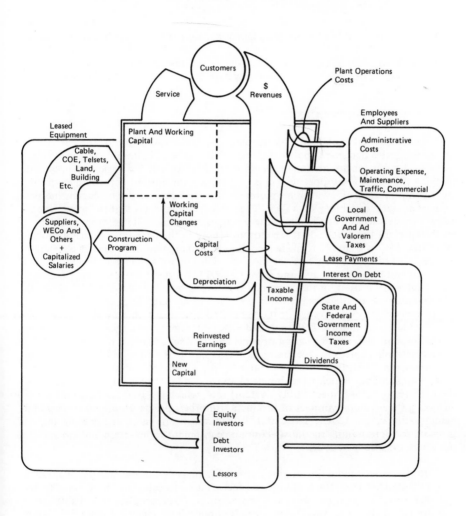

Figure 3

The second problem required to be addressed is the design of a decision support system or a set of tools to support Corporate Management in making reasoned and informed investment decisions. This would be the means by which the corporate staff would review, evaluate, and measure the various projects which are up for consideration.

A third requirement is a methodology for consolidating capital budget proposals.

A fourth function of Corporate Management is a review of major financial decisions. This could be viewed as a tracking system by which it will see the results of its decision process.

IV. THE SOLUTION PROCESS

While it has been explained why the anticipated reorganization of the company will necessitate a decision support system which will be considerably changed compared to the way we are now managing our business, one of the basic concepts in developing the decision support system is to integrate the current corporate environment and players in an evolutionary process. Figure 4 represents the current decision support analytic capability of AT&T. The three headings represent the areas where current models will be applicable if there is a restructuring. The acronyms underneath represent the models that are currently used in the corporate decision process. "EMPIRE TM" is a commercial financial modeling language. It is used as a general purpose tool in situations when "canned" models are not applicable. IF (Interactive Financial and Planning Model) and CIM (Capital Investment Model) are corporate type models; IF is used by the corporate planning group and CIM is a capital investment model used in analyses involving the study of accounting changes, depreciation changes, and asset evaluation. For the detariffed operations, there will be two models, CONTRAK (Contribution Tracking) and SERVAN (Service Analysis), which are general purpose models for evaluating projects and services to enable management to make economic choices by determing cash flows, rate of return and other financial measurements. "EMPIRE" will be useable by the detariffed operations for the same type of applications which were discussed above. Under the regulated operations is the EISS (Economic Impact Study System) tool, which is a Bell Laboratories tool for analyzing the economic impact of products from their pre-development through implementation stages. CUCRIT (Capital Utilization Criteria) is an engineering analysis program for determining the most economic equipment to maintain and enhance the telecommunications network.

With the above model library, the current Financial Management Organization is currently standardizing the methods and factors used to calculate the various financial measures, for example, taxes and depreciation. To accomplish this, a software package called the Core Analytic is currently under development. Figure 5 illustrates the role of the Core Analytic in the implementation of computational standards. Core Analytic will be a transferrable software package that will be integrated between the front-end and the output of various models just listed. The user input procedures, data structure and specialized pre-processing will be retained from the existing systems. CUCRIT will look like CUCRIT to its users; however, most of the analysis will be done by the Core Analytic. The outputs will look again like CUCRIT outputs to the users. The outputs needed for specific local management needs would be retained but with the provision that the specific information required by the

CURRENT DECISION SUPPORT
ANALYTIC CAPABILITY

MODEL LIBRARY		
Parent	Detariffed	Regulated
IF CIM "EMPIRE"	CONTRAK SERVAN "EMPIRE"	CUCRIT EISS

Figure 4

ROLE OF CORE ANALYTIC IN THE IMPLEMENTATION OF COMPUTATIONAL STANDARDS

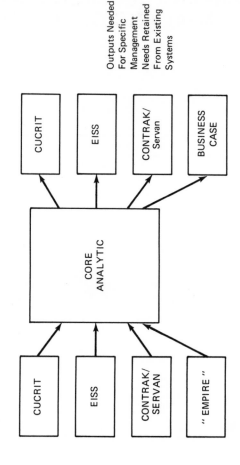

Figure 5

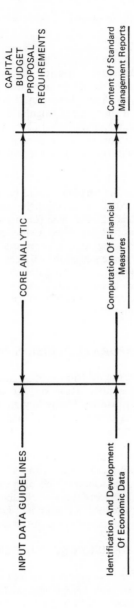

FINANCIAL MANAGEMENT ACTIVITIES SUPPORTING
PROJECT ECONOMIC EVALUATION PROCESS

Figure 6

financial decision organization will be generated. This will be the first step of the previously discussed standardization.

Carrying forward the concept of standards, which is a key supporting system, Figure 6 indicates the further eventual standardization that will be required throughout the project evaluation process. There should be standards for the primary input related to the specific project analysis. Also, there should be standards for use by the core analytic. The next step would then be the calculations within the Core Analytic. This will result in common financial calculations and outputs which will be formatted to meet the standard capital budget proposal report requirements. When this process has been completed, the first step in the decision support process will have been implemented.

Figure 7 illustrates the relation this first step could have in a decision support system process to the entire system. At the bottom of the figure, it is indicated that simple financial models using Core Analytic are used for initial project evaluation studies. This is the first step which was just described. Going up one level, the next step in the decision support system is an aggregation of products by lines of business. In the next step further aggregation and evaluation will occur when the lines of business are examined from an entity viewpoint. The final step deals with relationships from strategic and financial planning studies conducted on a corporate level. This is a framework that will provide for a gradual and logical transition from how we are now evaluating projects to the new requirements of the financial decision organization after restructuring.

V. INTEGRATION OF THE CORPORATE DECISION PROCESS

With Figure 7, the hierarchy of the decision process and the evolvment of the decision support system was briefly described. However, the corporate staff should integrate its operations with other key groups. The policy analysis function is really three-sided. One side is the evaluation of the lines of business. This can be defined as micro-planning and is the particular area which will be supported by the decision support system. The second leg of the triangle is the function which can be characterized as macro-planning. This function provides broad policy directions, constraints, and considerations in the micro-planning stage of the process. The third leg of the process is the capital generation from outside sources. This operation has to be performed in a dynamic manner correlated with the variability of business opportunities. How these three functions will interrelate in the decision support planning process will be shown in further detail as the decision support system is outlined.

VI. CURRENT VIEWS ON THE DECISION SUPPORT SYSTEM

Since no decision support system can be designed in a vacuum, it has been necessary to step through the events that have been occurring that suggest the possibility parts of the Bell System may be reorganized in order to give some idea how the ultimate system design will be tailored to fit the resulting environment. I am now getting down to the heart of the matter, a delineation of the specifications for a generic decision support system.

The first step regarding the Core Analytic has been discussed in some detail. As was stated, the Core Analytic is but one aspect in the direction of standardizing the

CONCEPTUAL HIERARCHY OF THE
PRODUCT ANALYSIS PROCESS

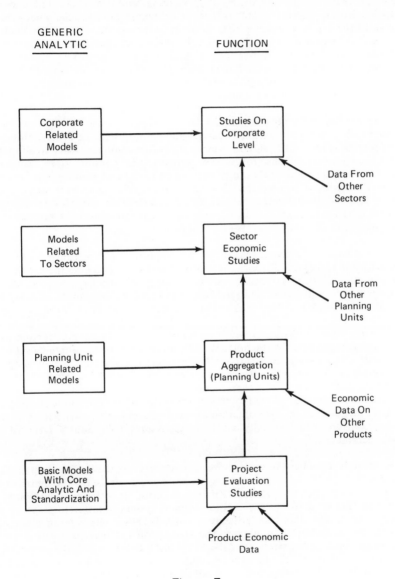

Figure 7

process and assumptions for analytical work performed by the entities and the Parent.

The second objective is the development of guidelines for producing and reviewing economic and financial evaluations of projects. In producing these guidelines, certain sub-objectives have evolved. One is that the economic and financial objectives must represent the lowest level for which the analysis for a particular business decision is practical. A second sub-objective is that the evaluations should be presented in the form of what is known as a base case. This will allow the corporate staff to make certain sensitivity analyses from a known base. The third sub-objective is that the level of information provided in a particular capital budget proposal should allow for comparison of alternatives within a given plan.

Another major objective is that the decision support system provide an analytical capability for the consolidation of capital budget proposals. To achieve this capability, the submission by entities should provide the information necessary to all management to investigate various groupings of projects. Prior consolidations within a capital budget proposal by entity should be performed to the extent necessary to minimize interactions with other projects. This will eliminate obvious cross elasticities at the lowest possible level. Another requirement in the decision support system, in regard to consolidation of capital budget proposals, is that information be provided to permit assessment of common costs and benefits.

A final major objective is that there be procedures for expert review of the capital budget proposals by the Parent. These procedures should include the capability for integration with various overall corporation policy and strategy analyses. Also to assist this review, a library of analytical decision support tools should be provided to support simulation and other analytical approaches at this level of the process.

The next step in this paper will show where the decision support system fits into the corporate picture. On the bottom of Figure 8, there is represented a set of planning units (PU), numbered 1 through N. Each one of these units will develop an individual request for funds together with the necessary supporting information. Just above the dashed line, that separates the entities from the Parent, is a box labeled "Standards." "Standards" will jointly be generated by the corporate staffing and organizations involved in the evaluation of economic and other environmental factors. This will ensure that the locally developed plans are synchronous in terms of those major parameters.

After unit plans have been developed, they will cross the line that separates the entities from the Parent for review, aggregation and analysis. On the figure to the left of that function, is a box labeled "Analytical Tools." It is this combination of analysis and tools that we define as the decision support system to differentiate it from the Core Analytic and other standardization work. Together with economic and other environmental condition inputs into the aggregation and analysis function, two other inputs are the long run strategy of the corporation developed by the corporate planning organization, and the financial planning necessary to perform the aggregation function. When the aggregation and analysis function is complete, the corporate staff will send the results to the Executive Office which either gives its approval, or requests that other information be developed. Another important information flow is from the financial decision organization to the economic and other environmental conditions generation and the capital planning functions. This can be illustrated with

INFORMATION FLOW

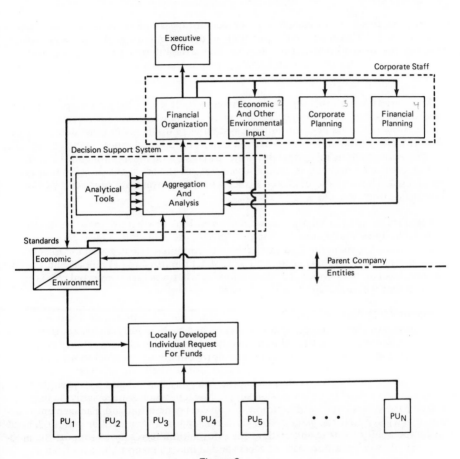

Figure 8

the following circumstances. If investment opportunities are such that they warrant further tapping of capital markets, even with higher rates, to provide the means of exploring additional appropriate business opportunities, the organization responsible for replanning of the capital needs will be sensitive to those needs indicated by the aggregation steps.

The next area to be discussed is the process for designing and building the decision support system. This is where the problems of design and integration are addressed. Basically, the design involves three factors; one is the internal aspects, a second is available state-of-the-art tools, and finally, there is the adhesive that will put the whole system together. These factors are illustrated in Figure 9.

There are three internal aspects that are important in the decision support system design process. Earlier in the paper, the functions and objectives for the corporate staff and the proposed decision support system were discussed in some detail. That is obviously a key internal aspect. A second important internal aspect is the current corporate environment as related to the earlier discussion of Figures 1 and 3. Finally, related to the environment, is the corporate state-of-the-art in the decision support system area. This was also discussed earlier when the current use of models by the three major organizations was reviewed.

Based on those internal aspects, we must now look at what are the state-of-the-art tools, techniques, and materials which we have to assemble into a decision support system. Basically, there are four categories; (1) computer languages and hardware; (2) data generation and management; (3) a model library; and (4) reports and graphics, The box labeled "Resources and Integration" is what was earlier referred to as the adhesive that will make all these things work together.

The tools (2) that are available and some broad considerations that are being used in the design of this decision support system will now be briefly discussed. In the language and hardware area, such things must be considered as the desirability of a high-level English-like language which allows non-programming personnel to develop appropriate models. Of course, it is necessary to look at the trade-offs between flexibility and ease of use. In the hardware area, the company has in place a large sophisticated computer capability, but the decision support system will not necessarily be initially limited to any particular configuration. In the data generation and management function, it is a given that the value of any decision support system will be greatly dependent on the ability to store and retrieve the information necessary to support the model library. A user must have ease of access and ability to manipulate data from a wide variety of sources, subject to legal constraints. The data base structure is, therefore, extremely important. The third technical consideration in designing the decision support system is the model library. The model library can be looked at as a variety of internally generated programs using corporate heuristics as well as an appropriate selection of mathematical algorithms. One example of the latter are econometric demand models. Other examples are simulation and mathematical programming software. In the reports and graphics area, there is a trite but true saying that a picture is worth a thousand words. (3) Such things as bubble charts, three-dimensional colored maps, and printed reports customized to appropriate levels of detail, are major magnets to attract executive involvement in the decision support framework and its eventual use.

DECISION SUPPORT SYSTEM PROCESS

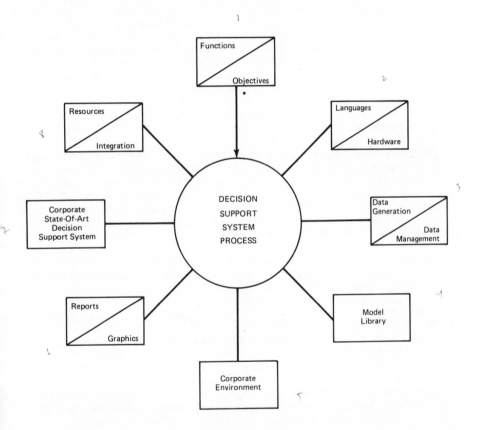

Figure 9

Going back to the information area, the decision support system will serve the purpose of synthesizing and interpreting information. The end result should be more information which has the content, and is in the form needed, for high-level management decision. It is viewed that the data base of the proposed decision support system will contain significant amounts of non-project information. An example is macro-economic (4) forecasts. Another type of information necessary to maintain any business is environmental information. Examples of this include the impact of consumer legislation, current trends in consumer action, major competitive processes, social change, and other factors that should be included in any overall corporate decision. Another type of necessary information is internally generated. An example of this is policy parameters set by upper management. The final example of the type of information that is necessary in a decision support system is operational. Line organizations much furnish information concerning productivity, costs and other appropriate line-generated data.

Decision Support Systems (5) represent the next step in the evolution of the management information system, a concept which lost favor because of high costs which were seldom translated into corresponding benefits. Where MIS was once thought of as a massive, comprehensive, corporate data base which could be accessed in any way by anybody, the decision support system approach emphasizes the availability of only necessary information and supplies the tools which are essential to utilize this information in a cost-effective manner.

Figure 10 is a representation of the likely decision support system. The start of the process is labeled "Individual Project Review." When the financial organization receives a planning unit proposal, it will know that a proposal has been developed using certain financial, economic and environmental standards. The financial organization's activities regarding any individual submission will involve a review in three aspects. To the right, the first review function is labeled "Cross Elasticity Analysis." This will insure that when lines of business are in different entities, projects are considered jointly by the Parent where there is a high degree of cross-elasticity between them. The next two steps would be in the nature of a filter operation; one is review of the economic measures and other key indicators and the second would be an evaluation of the riskiness of each proposal. There may be a corporate policy that states regardless of how profitable a situation looks, depending upon the bias of the downside risk, the corporattion may not wish to consider any particular project.

After a project has cleared its review as an individual project, the next step would involve initial aggregation and preliminary portfolio development. In this function, there will be consideration of such factors as economics of scale. Another objective will be to review the aggregation in terms of strategic considerations. This would include considerations of competitive status, technological strengths, objectives and risk attitudes. Another input into the portfolio development would be the evaluation of projects and their groupings in terms of the corporate structure. An example of this would be that consideration be given to the production process regarding vertical integration and economies of scale.

Historically in the Bell System, product design has been aimed at building the absolute highest quality into a product and guaranteeing every customer almost immediate service. In developing portfolios, the evaluating of alternative individual investments will have to take into account that different and difficult balances will have to

DECISION SUPPORT SYSTEM

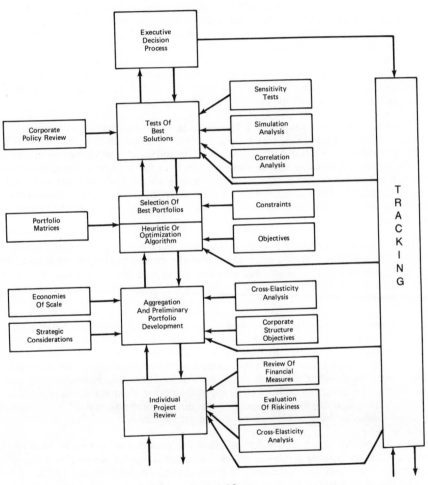

Figure 10

be struck to perpetuate the tradition of product reliability and service excellence. Another consideration that will go into the aggregation solution relates to the marketing mix. (6) Such factors as promotion, advertising and distribution are variables that must be considered in the development of any portfolio.

A potential useful feature of the decision support system is the ability to support the best set of portfolios. (There will obviously be many non-quantifiable factors considered in relation to the analytical results.) (7) This could be accomplished by use of either heuristic models or an optimization algorithm. A mathematical programming model, with necessary constraints objectives and with various objective functions, is one possibility. A possible heuristic model may be based on what is called "portfolio matrices." (8) Such matrices develop portfolios based on indices concerning such elements as growth, profitability, the cyclicalness of the product, inflation, impact resistance, and worldwide scope concerning the various alternatives.

After the set of best proposals is developed these best portfolios will be run through a series of tests. One test to be considered is a "simulation analysis." (9) This activity would develop the statistics necessary to reduce the set of best solutions to a final selection. Also, there will be more sensitivity tests to provide measures of relative risk between the best portfolios. Another type of risk analysis is called correlation analysis. (10) For example, if all, or a majority, of the projects in a particular portfolio were sensitive to the high cost of energy, that particular portfolio might be rejected.

If the above is feasible and understandable by management, a next step might be to take the resulting data and insert them into the executive decision process. In this process, questions may be asked and this may require additional analysis. You will note on Figure 10 that there are arrows going both directions between all of the major functions.

The information flow line going out of the executive decision process represents that a decision has been made and that a particular plan has been put into action. After being put into action, the long block to the right, labeled "Tracking," is the feedback mechanism that measure how well the plan is achieving its stated objectives. The current view is that the above processes will have timeframes several years into the future. One must remember key items of telephone plant often last more than 25 years. The planning horizon aspect of the timing conventions will be an important design element in the proposed decision support system.

It is hoped that this broad-scaled overview has provided some idea of what the proposed decision support system may look like. This is just an outline; the stage of development obviously limits the level of detail that can be presented. The Core Analytic and the integration of the core into the standard financial models of the corporation is scheduled to be operating shortly. The work outlined in Figure 10 is preceeding parallel to the Core Analytic. The individual project review, aggregation and preliminary portfolio analysis, and parts of the tracking system also should be in place soon. These are believed to be essential goals to ensure a smooth transition and effective operation of the restructured Bell System. There will undoubtedly be changes in the ultimate design and as to where optimization is possible and in the detail of analytical testing.

VII. FORESEEN PROBLEMS

Admittedly, the program outlined is ambitious, but when one looks at the size, diversity and complexity of the Bell System, the challenge is to design a decision support system which capitalizes on the state-of-the-art and balances this against the ability of management to utilize such a tool. It is realized that there are technical problems regarding the state-of-the-art, timeframes given for development, and the resources available. Fortunately, the corporation has available a sophisticated group of professionals with expertise in the development, implementation and operation of systems of this scope.

As in any business, one of the basic considerations in the decision support system is to design it so it is not one computer program under the control of one organization. This would be both naive and impractical. It is believed that the proposed design will provide an environment that meets the needs of the important groups while complying with anticipated regulatory information flow constraints.

Another problem with such a system is that of economics. Such elements as development, maintenance, and operating costs must be considered.

Finally, in a large organization such as AT&T there are often problems in the implementation of a large system such as this. Determining who has responsibility for central coordination and responsibility for the project can cause critical difficulties. History has shown, however, that AT&T executives are very successful in resolving this type of problem.

FOOTNOTES

(1)   *Engineering Economy – A Manager's Guide to Decision Making,* Third Edition, McGraw-Hill, 1977

(2)   "DSS: An Executive Mind Support System," P.G. Keen and G.R. Wagner, *Datamation,* November 1979.

(3)   "Economic Analysis Through Color Graphics," Marnie Samuelson, *Computer Graphics World,* October 1980

(4)   "Decision Support Systems For Corporate Planning," Otto Eckstein, prepared for 1/22/81 joint NASCP/TIMS seminar entitled "Use of Models in Corporate Planning."

(5)   *Management Decision Support Systems,* Andrew M. McCosh and Michael S. Scott Morton, John Wiley and Sons, 1978

(6)   "Decision Support Systems for Marketing Managers," John D.C. Little, *Journal of Marketing,* Summer 1979

(7)   *Capital Budgeting – Planning and Control of Capital Expenditures,* John J. Clark, Thomas J. Hindelang, Robert E. Pritchard, Prentice-Hall, Inc., 1979

(8)   "Designing Product and Business Portfolios," Yoram Wind and Vijay Mahajan, *Harvard Business Review,* January-February 1981.

(9)   "Evaluating Risk – Sensitivity Analysis and Simulation," Jerry W. Durway, *Infosystems,* May 1979.

(10)   "Mathematical Programming, The Capital Asset Pricing Model and Capital Budgeting of Interrelated Projects," H.F. Thompson, *The Journal of Finance,* March 1976

DECISION SUPPORT SYSTEMS
M.J. Ginzberg, W. Reitman, E.A. Stohr (editors)
North-Holland Publishing Company
© *DSS, 1982*

APPLYING ARTIFICIAL INTELLIGENCE TO DECISION SUPPORT: WHERE DO GOOD ALTERNATIVES COME FROM?

by
Walter Reitman
Graduate School of Business Administration
New York University

ABSTRACT

Current decision support systems provide the user with a context for specifying possible courses of action. They enable the user to project a scenario beginning from that action, and to estimate its likely consequences. It is still up to the user, however, to determine each specific alternative to be assessed. By contrast, the decision support provided by a human staff goes much further. In particular, the staff is responsible for developing a small set of good alternatives: the decision maker does not have to search through the space of all possible actions himself.

Where do these good alternatives come from? Can we program the skills required for finding them? AI systems for this already exist in several tactical and strategic planning contexts. Using as an example an artificial intelligence system that develops good moves from the game of Go, we examine the means by which such systems set up plausible goals, ascertain available resources, locate constraints, match resources to options, and thereby restrict search to very small subsets of good alternatives. To the extent that the concepts and techniques underlying such programs are applicable in the MIS context, they open up the possibility of augmenting substantially the effectiveness of decision support systems.

1. INTRODUCTION TO ARTIFICIAL INTELLIGENCE

Artificial intelligence (AI) is a field at the intersection of computer science, cognitive psychology, logic, linguistics, and mathematics. Its concern is intelligent programs. The scope of AI concepts, techniques, and systems applicable or potentially applicable to business problems is quite broad. We cite a few examples to illustrate this scope.

● Natural Language Inquiry

Artificial intelligence systems capable of written natural language communication were first developed about a decade ago. More recently, several firms have developed restricted natural language query programs for use as front-ends for data base systems. These systems, which are potentially also a first step toward spoken natural language inquiry, are now undergoing intensive testing to evaluate their commercial potential.

● Input Monitoring and Error Control Procedures

Reducing input error is a basic MIS concern. The standard procedures for this, e.g., range and membership checking, are instances of one general principle: the more relevant knowledge you can bring to bear, the more likely you are to detect erroneous entries. AI knowledge-representation techniques allow us to realize this principle in more powerful forms, i.e., in general knowledge-based input-monitoring systems.

● Learning and Training

AI investigators have developed and implemented comprehensive theories of the processes involved in learning complex skills, including problem-solving skills. Such implementations can provide simulated worlds in which these skills may be learned and exercised.

● Automatic Design and Debugging

Recently, there have been a number of advances in creating AI systems capable of constraint-driven design, e.g., of electronic circuits. Systems also have been developed for detecting design bugs. These bug detection systems add considerable power to our ability to automate the design process.

● Systems Management

Research is currently under way on intelligent control strategies for complex systems. Such work typically involves programming (1) a model of the system to be managed; (2) functions for analyzing sensed system conditions with respect to the model; and (3) planning and control functions that come up with appropriate actions for the current system situation.

● Conceptually-organized Data Bases

The data base systems now available model a rather limited set of relations among elements. Artificial intelligence is concerned with the general design principles underlying more sophisticated and powerful representations. Several such systems have been developed on an experimental basis.

● Robotics

Industrial robots are now an important factor of production in several major fields. Current work in AI focuses on a variety of avenues for improving robots' capacity for intelligent action. Examples include: improving perceptual capabilities, thereby permitting appropriate response to a wider range of situational changes; and improving the ability to plan actions given incomplete information and the need to acquire additional relevant data.

2. SOME LIMITATIONS OF CURRENT DECISION SUPPORT SYSTEMS

The particular AI concepts and techniques described below are of interest because they are potentially useful as tools for augmenting current approaches to decision support.

A modern decision support system provides its users with three things: a context for specifying possible actions; a mechanism for projecting the consequences of those actions; and a means of evaluating the results. Good decision support systems are powerful tools now. Yet compared with the support provided by a competent human staff, they are still very limited. Many decision problems involve *interactions* among intelligent agencies or organizations. Current decision support systems cannot deal with these directly. Instead, their projection mechanisms typically require that these interacting intelligences be replaced by numerical models. These, it is hoped, will approximate the consequences of the interactions as the system moves through time. More important, still, even with the best current decision support systems, it remains up to the user to specify explicitly each of the individual alternatives to be considered.

Contrast this with a sampling of the issues we would expect to be considered when decision support is provided by a good old-fashioned human staff.

- What are our goals?
- What have we got to work with?
- What are the constraints?
- What alternatives are likely to be worth investigating?
- How do they work out?
- How do actions that advance one goal affect our ability to achieve others?
- Whom do we have to deal with, and what are their goals, resources, and constraints?

To make our view of the current status of decision support systems more concrete, let's look at a page from recent history.

One month before his inauguration in January, 1977, Jimmy Carter received a memo fron Patrick Caddell, his personal decision support system. According to Broder (1977), the Caddell memo tried to anticipate likely sources of opposition to the prospective Carter programs and to work out strategy for dealing with them. The memo was concerned mainly with the Democratic left. This is because Caddell saw the growing population of college-educated white collar and professional workers as a group that would have to be attracted to the Democrats if the party were to be successful in the future. Caddell felt that the actions best suited to attracting this group would cause rumblings from the left. To cope with this problem, Caddell suggested a series of countermeasures. These included some of the symbolic gestures of Carter's first 100 days, and the policy of co-opting allies from the left by appointment to middle-level positions in the new administration. Once you have read this memo, Broder observes, "almost everything (Carter) has done as President makes sense."

How are analyses such as Caddell's possible when there are so many factors to be considered, and when any prediction about the behavior of an individual or a group seems hardly more than an informed guess? A sceptic might wonder whether the memo shows anything about decision making at all. Caddell's prescience may be more apparent than real. The memo may simply restate ideas previously agreed upon. Perhaps there also are drawers full of other memos, memos dealing with worlds no one will ever see.

Though such a sceptic would be right about the weaknesses of the memo as evidence, that is not the point. For anyone familiar with complex decision making in business and government, the memo rings true. These are the ways decision support staff proceed in such situations. These are the kinds of things they try to do.

A good human decision support staff has two jobs to do. First it must reduce the set of all possible actions to the few that look potentially realistic, feasible, and good. It is this small handful that the top level decision maker actually considers when he reaches his final decision. Second, both in winnowing through the alternatives, and in projecting their consequences, the staff somehow must deal directly with the inter-relations among the various parties involved. This is the only way it can hope to apply its knowledge about the parties, their goals, their resources, and the constraints under which they must operate. In general, however, we simply do not yet know how to in-corporate such knowledge in numerical projection models. As a result, there is a real ceiling to what we can expect of decision support systems cast in current molds.

If we are willing to entertain this view of present day decision support systems and their limitations, how might we go about trying to break out of current molds? One tack might be to look at some related work in artificial intelligence and to explore the possibilities for arbitrage. The balance of this paper is intended in this vein. The work described, a program for playing Go, makes no claim to practical applicability in its present form. But as an artificial intelligence system, it works very well, and the principles underlying it may point the way toward more powerful decision support designs.

3. THE WORLD OF GO*

Go is a protracted oriental board game that emphasizes long range strategy. What exactly does "protracted" mean? Kawabata, the Nobel-prize-winning Japanese author, has organized an entire novel around a single famous game that continued through some fourteen sessions and lasted altogether about forty hours. Modern games be-tween Go professionals are much shorter, usually taking on the order of twelve hours, but even these time spans afford ample opportunity for the strategic analysis and planning central to the game.

Nothing in the United States approaches the intellectual status and impact Go has in the Orient. In Japan, newspapers compete to sponsor Go tournaments and report the results. Significant matches are presented live on national TV, with commentators providing instant analyses to bridge long pauses between moves. The winnings of Go professionals compare with those of top tennis and golf pros in the United States. In fact, the cultural significance of Go in Japan is perhaps most like that of physical sports in this country. Just as sports metaphor spills over into economic and political activity here, so it is with Go in the Orient. Boorman (1969) for example, claims that Maoist revolutionary strategy can best be understood in terms of Mao's familiarity with the tactical and strategic precepts of Go, and Go is even supposed to have been part of the required training for Japanese naval officers prior to World War II.

The general influence of Go thinking in the modern Japanese business world also is easy to discern. Business firms are strong supporters of professional Go. Outstand-ing players are regularly asked to present series of lectures on Go tactics and strategy to company personnel. And Japanese institutional image campaigns regularly include advertisements showing the company president pondering a particular knotty prob-lem on the Go board. The extend to which Go metaphor and precepts actually guide strategic thinking in business planning is much more difficult for an outsider to assess. Nonetheless, as we consider the various explanations that have been offered for Japan's economic effectiveness — the ability to find harmonious solutions for con-flicting interests, the concern for doing things right the first time, and the emphasis on

the long run implications of decisions, the similarities to the essentials of good Go
thinking are striking.

Here, of course, our main concern is not with Go as a tool for training good managers, but with Go as a testbed for developing more powerful frameworks for decision support. We need, therefore, to say something about the actual structure of the
game. This will enable us to follow our decision support system in operation. Then,
when we are done, we can examine the possibilities of applying the underlying principles to practical decision support domains.

4. THE STRUCTURE OF GO

Go as we have seen involves substantial amounts of tactical and strategic analysis
and planning. It is, ultimately, a contest for territory between two players, black and
white. Figure 1 shows a Go game in progress. As the figure indicates, the game is
played on the 361 intersections of a 19 x 19 grid. The two players alternate turns.
Each turn consists of placing a stone of the appropriate color at some point on the
board. Unless it is captured, the stone remains on that point for the entire game. The
unnumbered black circles in the figure represent handicap stones given to black at the
start of the game. The numbered black and white circles show the order of moves.
Since no stones have been captured, the figure as a whole also shows the current state
of the game immediately following white's move 45 at B10.

Go game in progress

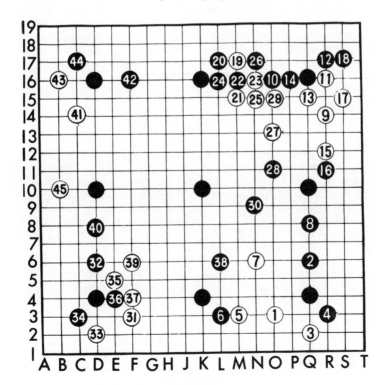

Figure 1

A player kills (captures) an enemy stone and removes it from the board whenever he succeeds in surrounding the stone. Direct capture of a single stone is not a very profitable idea in itself, however. The possibility of capture is significant mainly because it gives rise to moves that threaten important higher-order units.

The Go program recognizes a variety of higher order units. A string consists of a single isolated stone or two or more stones of the same color located on immediately adjacent grid points. Two strings of the same color, in close proximity, with no intervening enemy stones, are considered by the program to be connected together by a linkage.

Linked strings form groups, which may enclose territory. Groups usually are attacked and defended as units, not string by string. The extent and degree of prospective territorial control exercised by each side is a function of the relative stability of each side's groups and the interacting dispositions of the two sets of groups over the board. Each group may be thought of as having associated with it a set of options. These are general ways in which that particular group may be developed, protected, and used. As a single move may serve multiple functions, a play at one point, in addition to affecting the options in its immediate area, also may augment, modify, or reduce the options of groups elsewhere on the board.

Go games typically run 200 moves or more, and each turn offers on average close to 250 legal plays. Brown and Dowsey (1971) estimate the number of different possible games of Go at about 10^{700}, compared with 10^{120} for chess, and they point out that exhaustive Go search only three moves deep would entail generating and evaluating about 8,000,000 whole-board positions. Yet videotaped game records presented by Kerwin and Reitman (1973) show that in the course of making their decisions, advanced amateur players can look 30 moves ahead; the published literature contains still deeper lookahead sequences. As this suggests, the analysis of future possibilities during decision-making in Go must be a highly focused, goal-driven, constructive process.

5. GO PROGRAM DATA STRUCTURES AND CONTROL FLOW

We've suggested in Section 2 that if we compared the support provided by present day decision support systems with that provided by human staff, the most important difference is in the staff's ability to come up with good alternatives. Abstractly considered, the issue is one of effective search. This is particularly true within the framework of conventional decision theory. There, all alternatives are assumed to be given, and the problem is reduced to finding needles in haystacks. But this is simply inappropriate metaphor. As Simon (1959) pointed out more than two decades ago, alternatives are not given; they must be constructed.

Thus, as we examine our AI system in what follows, what we want to understand is not how it "searches" for good alternatives among the bad ones, but how it controls the process of designing the alternatives. This is how it creates good alternatives, and avoids wasting effort on bad ones.

To understand how this is achieved, let's begin with the top level flow of control. The Go program [1, 2] consists of three components: DESCRIBE, CONSTRUCT, and PROJECT. DESCRIBE and CONSTRUCT alternate; this defines the basic program cycle. Whenever it is the program's turn to play, it first analyzes and DESCRIBEs the situation resulting from the opponent's most recent move. Then, using that description, it CONSTRUCTs and evaluates move alternatives. This DESCRIBE–CONSTRUCT cycle determines the program's next move.

PROJECT is called by DESCRIBE and CONSTRUCT whenever they need to know the likely outcome of a particular line of play. When PROJECT is called, it is given a specific objective and a specific initial move in the service of that objective. Taking these as its starting point, PROJECT extrapolates the most likely hypothetical move sequences that might be expected to follow. It also evaluates the local outcome of each sequence. In other words, PROJECT generates scenarios. It attempts to answer the question: what happens if we start with this objective and make this move. There are two PROJECT subcomponents. The first (Reitman and Wilcox, 1979b) estimates tactical consequences. The second (Lehner, 1981) uses a representative search procedure to bypass tactical issues and focus on strategic consequences.

Figures 2 and 3 outline the structures of DESCRIBE and CONSTRUCT. The figures are highly simplified. In particular, PROJECT, the lookahead subsystem, is called from a great many points other than those shown.

Referring to these two figures, let's now follow out the flow of control through the two-part cycle in somewhat more detail. First, immediately following a play by either side, DESCRIBE updates all those elements of GAMEMAP, the program's multilevel representation of the situation, affected by the latest move. Next, if it is the program's turn to play, CONSTRUCT chooses a move.

THE STRUCTURE OF THE <u>DESCRIBE</u> COMPONENT

⬤ Update representations of:

- Strings

- Lenses

- Links

- Groups

- Webs

- Sector lines

- Territories

⬤ Update tactical analyses, using **PROJECT**

⬤ Update stability estimates for all groups

Figure 2

THE STRUCTURE OF THE <u>CONSTRUCT</u> COMPONENT

● Deal with any locally urgent problems, e.g., by

    Attacking or defending a vital string

● If there are no locally urgent problems: Try to develope a friendly group, using experts for

- Killing cutting strings

- Extending towards and squeezing an enemy group

- Counterattacking

- Crossing sector lines

- Stabilizing a friendly potential territory

- Running to a friendly group

● If there are no good moves for developing a friendly group: Try to attack an enemy group, using experts for

- Attacking the group's vital shape points (this may entail a call to **PROJECT**)

- Squeezing the group's development space

- Enclosing the group

● If there are no good moves for attacking an enemy group:
Call midgame functions

● If there are no good midgame moves:
Call endgame functions

Figure 3

GAMEMAP is indexed through a set of interrelated GAMEBOARDS. Each board is an array that points to all data structures of a particular type. Some boards, e.g., STRINGBOARD and LINKBOARD, index the basic game elements at the various levels (strings, linkages, groups, territories, and potential territories). In Figure 1, for example, looking up the board point B8 in the LINKBOARD array enables any program function to access the data structure representing the linkage from the D8 string to the left edge of the board. Other boards, e.e., LENSBOARD, WEBBOARD, SECTORBOARD, and TACTICSBOARD, index elements analogous to those in a skilled Go player's perceptual and cognitive representation of the current situation. Lenses represent and monitor local stone patterns. Web data structures are surrogates for certain kinds of visual scanning. Webs follow the external configurations of groups, radiating out and indexing and detecting changes occurring around individual groups. Sector lines, e.g., the one between B10 and C14, correspond to those looser relations among stones that dynamically divide the board into tenuously defined regions. These sector barriers help define potential territories and strategic threats to groups. Finally, the TACTICSBOARD indexes tactical data structures associated with individual strings, linkages, and significant board points. These data structures record the results of analyses produced by calls to PROJECT, the entry point to the subsystem responsible for all lookahead. This is selective, best-first lookahead. Each such analysis answers some specific tactical question about the associated element. The resulting tactical data structure is maintained unless invalidated by subsequent moves that affect strings or board points involved in the analysis, at which point PROJECT reanalyzes the situation.

6. UPDATING THE REPRESENTATION AFTER A MOVE

To fix ideas, consider the situation shown in Figure 1, ignoring the order of play. As soon as white plays move 45 at B10, MOVE is called to update GAMEMAP selectively. Only structures directly or indirectly impacted by the move are affected. UPDATE.STRINGS sets up a string data structure representing B10. Now UPDATE. - LENSES creates a lens to monitor any future board changes around the pattern formed by white B10 and black D10.

Subsequent DESCRIBE functions update other units in a similar fashion. UPDATE.GROUPS modifies existing group data structures and creates new ones. After a group data structure for B10 has been created, UPDATE.WEBS creates a web data structure indexing the board points surrounding B10. The web reaches out to the white group at B16 and C14, the open area around E12 and E13, and the black group beginning at D10 and running down toward the bottom of the board. These web data structures may be used by any CONSTRUCT functions considering attacks on adjacent enemy groups, or defensive plays running a group toward friendly groups or out into unoccupied areas. UPDATE.SECTOR.LINES creates a data structure representing an imaginary line running from B10 to C14. This sector line is used by UPDATE.TERRITORIES to create a potential territory data structure corresponding to the area bounded by the two white groups on the left of the board.

Now UPDATE.TACTICAL.ANALYSES calls PROJECT to assess the tactical status of strings and linkages created or potentially affected by the most recent play. No actual lookahead is required for the B10 string, which is found to be tactically secure on the basis of context information from GAMEMAP. When contextual information is insufficient for a decision, PROJECT may generate lookahead sequences

running from a few hypothetical board positions to 50 or more. Finally, UPDATE. -
GROUP.STABILITY. ESTIMATES rates stability for the B10 group.

HOW DESCRIBE WORKS

● Purpose: creates and maintains a *detailed, accurate, up-to-date representation* of
the current situation

● What DESCRIBE produces:

• A *multilevel* representation of the situation

• Identifies lower level elements (e.g., strings, links) used in *tactical analyses*

• Identifies higher level elements (e.g., groups, potential territories) used in
strategic planning

• Provides local *situational contexts* for all elements

• Analyzes and describes *interrelations* and *interactions* among elements

● Principles of operation:

• Works from *knowledge of the basic element types* (strings, links, groups, etc.)
and of their possible interrelations

• Constructs higher level elements by *analyzing interrelations* among their
lower level components

• *Reduces updating computation* by using knowledge of structural barriers
that restrict interactions among elements

Figure 4

As summarized in Figure 4, DESCRIBE and its subfunctions serve at least three
vital purposes. They carry out, at progressively higher levels, the aggregation, analysis,
and local interrelating of the patterns and structures representing the game situation.
Thus they provide the basic elements the CONSTRUCT functions deal with. They
maintain the data base that allows the CONSTRUCT functions to deal with each element in context. This enables the program to locate interactions and find moves that
do several jobs at once, Finally, DESCRIBE updating corrects the representation
after each play, deriving its immediate implications at every level it affects. This is
how the program determines exactly all the immediate consequences of its own
moves, and those of its opponent.

7. CHOOSING THE PROGRAM'S MOVE

Returning now to Figure 3, CONSTRUCT steps through an ordered list of functions and accepts the first move returned from them. LOCAL.URGENT and its sub-

functions are responsible for dealing with any urgent problems that may have arisen as a consequence of the immediately preceding black-white move pair. If there are none, control passes to DEVELOP.GROUP. This function, working both with the group stability data computed under DESCRIBE, and with assessments of the values of each of the program's groups, selects the friendly group it considers to be most worth developing. It then invokes its subfunctions in the order shown in the figure. Each has information about a class of developmental options, the conditions under which these options are appropriate, and the means available for realizing them.

If there are no valuable friendly groups in need of development, control passes to ATTACK.GROUP. This function considers the various enemy groups, again ordered by value and stability, and attempts through its subfunctions to generate suitable attacking moves against its target. If there are no attackable enemy groups, control passes to the remaining midgame and endgame functions.

Figure 5 shows the basic principles underlying the development of move alternatives. The process proceeds from general problems and options to more specific ones. The system relies on the experts at each level to know a good deal about the options available there. This has two consequences. First, usually only the best few possibilities at any level are considered. Second, if higher level experts have chosen properly, then lower levels also need only consider the best more specific options. There may be other considerations at a lower level that might improve the final choice there, but that is the responsibility of the critics at that level. Since the functions at each level generally provide an ordered set of choices, the critics have alternatives to work with. And if the situation changes, so that the specific low-level objective no longer has priority, both the situational change and its immediate implications are picked up on the next pass through the DESCRIBE–CONSTRUCT cycle.

HOW CONSTRUCT WORKS

- Purpose: to create *good* alternatives

- Organized as a *top-down multilevel system of experts*

- Assigns *priorities to situations* based upon *urgency* and *importance*

- Considers options at each level in *best-first* order

- Works from the global, abstract, and general to the specific

- Uses *experts-and-critics* structure to generate and test alternatives
  Plans and *planning* are *responsive* to changing/situational conditions

Figure 5

8. USING PROJECT TO CREATE SCENARIOS

The DESCRIBE–CONSTRUCT system just presented structures its data into a coherent multilevel representation of elements and their interrelations. Using this representation it focuses upon problems of primary importance, and poses specific questions about future possibilities with respect to these problems.

The PROJECT subsystem is responsible for taking such questions and answering them, using lookahead where necessary. We have seen, however, that a search space the size of that in Go makes general lookahead impossible. How then does PROJECT manage to control its lookahead sufficiently to achieve its results?

A simplified overview of the processing flow for the PROJECT selective lookahead system is presented in Figure 6. The main questions PROJECT asks at each iteration in the lookahead process are shown in Figure 7. In Go, as in many real world problem domains, the problem solver does not have full control over the changes that are made in the situation he is dealing with. The opponent's moves also change the situation , generally in ways intended to thwart the objectives of the problem solver. A system meant to analyze future possibilities in such a domain must include means for ascertaining and coping with the effects of one side's actions on the plans and goals of the other. In the hypothetical world that is created or further extended at each PROJECT iteration, this is the responsibility of ENTRY.FAIL?. This function, which calls RESUME.GOAL and RESULT.FAIL?. checks for and tries to correct any urgent new problems that may have resulted from the other side's most recent hypothetical move.

RESUME.GOAL is responsible for determining whether to truncate some line of exploration and instead reinstate some prior higher-level goal. It keeps lookahead focused on the most urgent aspect of a problem. RESULT.FAIL? is called by ENTRY.FAIL? whenever, owing to a failure of some kind for the side on move, search returns to a previously generated hypothetical board position. RESULT.FAIL? makes use of information about prior failure. It will prefer those options that deal explicitly with the source of the immediately preceding failure.

PROJECT'S PROCESSING FLOW

- Begins with an initial situation, an initial goal, and a proposed action
- Develops a goal-and-subgoals structure and iterates over it
- Chooses an appropriate action for the side on move
- Makes the move hypothetically, then reiterates, from the modified position, for the opposing side
- Continues iterating and making subsequent hypothetical moves for the two sides until the sequence of moves is successful for one side or the other
- Backs up to a significant choice point, and begins a new plausible (sub-)sequence from that point
- When a sufficient number of these plausible action sequences have been constructed, uses the outcomes from this set of scenarios to draw a plausible conclusion about the likely result of attempting to achieve the initial goal from the initial situation

Figure 6

KNOWLEDGE-BASED QUESTIONS ASKED BY <u>PROJECT</u> AT EACH ITERATION

- Is there a more urgent higher-level goal that applies to this modified situation? If so, the current subgoal structure below that higher-level goal is truncated

- Are there constraints to be added to the current goal as a consequence of prior failures?

- Can the goal be rejected out of hand, without search?

- Would some subgoal of the current goal be more appropriate?

- What type of action is most appropriate to the current goal in its situational context?

- Does the action check out to be satisfactory?

Figure 7

RESOURCES collects information about the means available on the board for pursuing the current goal. Some of these data are obtained directly from GAMEMAP. Others are computed with the help of lookahead surrogates.

There is no point wasting lookahead on a goal that can be rejected out of hand without it, so once the RESOURCES information is available, GOAL.FAIL? uses it to assess the reasonableness of the current goal. This is an example of the use of surrogates instead of actual lookahead. The use of surrogates *avoids* search wherever possible, thereby keeping the search tree as restricted as possible. In this sense, the lookahead system succeeds because it tries to be a lookahead *avoidance* system whenever it can.

Next, SUBGOAL chooses among the various general methods available for achieving a goal of a given type. It does this by checking the precondition sets associated with each option to see which are satisfied in the current board and goal contexts. Given an acceptable goal and the move candidates supplied by RESOURCES, GOAL.-REPLY and REPLY.FAIL? make various checks designed to maximize the effectiveness of the move selected with respect to the current board situation. If a line fails, BACKUP.FAIL? decides whether anything further can be done in the current board position, i.e., by backing up to some antecedent goal.

In summary, as indicated in Figure 8, every PROJECT lookahead is intended to answer a specific question, e.g., about the tactical security of a string or linkage, posed by the function invoking PROJECT. PROJECT records its results for each such element in a tactical data structure. This is maintained as part of GAMEMAP until the analysis is called into question by some subsequent move.

Successful selective lookahead in the Go program also is the result of several other factors. The program's multilevel representation enables it to move back and forth between general objectives and local problems. Thus it is able to do abstract analysis, which drastically reduces search, without losing contact with concrete implementation details. The representation also enables PROBE to restrict search spatially. The board area searched is not rigidly circumscribed, and may be expanded dynamically to include relevant points anywhere. But only a small subset of the 361 board points, typically 10 percent or less, will be involved in any given probe. Finally, PROJECT uses knowledge-based techniques to constrain the growth of its goal structures, it substitutes lookahead surrogates for search whenever it can, and makes effective use of information about past failures to improve subsequent search.

HOW PROJECT WORKS

● Purpose: to *create* and *evaluate* specific, likely *scenarios*

● It is *goal-driven,* and tries to answer *specific questions*

● Works with full, explicit *representations* of problems and situations, not with numeric estimates or summaries of their *values*

● Uses prior *abstract knowledge* and *analysis* provided by DESCRIBE and CONSTRUCT

● Permits *dynamic redefinition* of the set of relevant facts

● Uses surrogates to *avoid* detailed projection wherever possible, thereby cutting down the amount of computation and search

● Uses information about past failures to *refine* search objectives and constraints

● *Samples likeliest* scenarios, then *generalizes*

● Provides tactical analyses and results that can be *saved*; this results in:

  ● Computational *economy* and *selectivity*

  ● *Sensitivity* to significant changes in (pre-) conditions

  ● Immediate grasp of the *meanings* of such changes

  ● Ability to exploit emerging interactions and opportunities *as they arise*

Figure 8

9. PROGRAM IMPLEMENTATION AND PERFORMANCE

The Go program is written in LISP/MTS and runs on the AMDAHL/470. It compiles into about 330k words, uses about six cpu seconds per black-white pair of moves, and creates about 86 hypothetical board position per move pair. For additional information, see Reitman and Wilcox (1979a, 1979b).

As assessed in games against human opponents, the program produces sustained play serving reasonable goals at approximately the level of a knowledgeable beginner. To provide a finer measure of PROJECT performance in particular, 278 PROJECT outcomes were randomly selected from two test games. Almost 40 percent utilized only contextual information and involved no actual generation of hypothetical moves. The remaining cases are divided into three classes by problem difficulty. As indicated in Figure 9, PROJECT answers almost 88 percent of the easy problems correctly. Faced with moderately difficult problems, the program comes up with the right answer 56 percent of the time. There are only three cases altogether in the difficult category, but the program does get them right. For all three classes, the search tree branching factor is about 1.2. In other words PROJECT controls the expansion of the search so tightly that, on average, there are only 1.2 nodes descending from any given node in the search tree. This figure incidentally, is very close to that found in lookahead data from highly skilled human Go players.

Note also that PROJECT's conclusions were scored correct only if it returned the right answer for the right reason, i.e., only if the program explored all the critical paths and came up with a correct initial move. Thus the base chance expectation against which these results should be evaluated is something very close to zero.

HOW WELL DOES PROJECT WORK?

● Empirical analysis:

- ● Easy problems, 88% correct

- ● Moderately difficult problems, 56% correct

- ● Difficult problems, 100% correct

● Interpreting the results:

- ● Maintains control over search-space size

- ● Branching factor held to 1.2

- ● Baseline expectation of correct solution is essentially zero

Figure 9

10.   APPLICABILITY TO PRACTICAL DECISION SUPPORT

We noted in Section 2 of this paper some limitations of current decision support systems. We suggested that because they cannot make use of knowledge about goals, resources, options, and constraints in an interactive framework, they are unable to selectively generate good alternatives. They can only project forward, in a non-interactive, non-selective fashion, the outcomes of options chosen for consideration by a human user. By contrast, the work discussed in the preceding sections demonstrates that a program *can* collect, organize, and use such knowledge in ways that enable it to create good alternatives entirely on its own. Yet, since the domain is Go, the value of the demonstration is only that of an existence proof. It has no practical utility as it stands.

Can we use the general principles described above as the basis for more powerful decision support systems for business? If so, how long is it likely to be before we have systems that can selectively construct good alternatives in areas of practical concern?

One approach to answering such questions is to look at the record. We can refer back to the artificial intelligence applications summarized in Section 1 and ask about the length of the development process in those cases. If we take natural language front ends as an example, we see that more than a decade has elasped between the first significant "existence proof" programs and the development of commercial applications. Time spans for the other applications mentioned in Section 1 are, very roughly, on the same order.

The manager who is not a computer specialist may find this hard to understand. Software is software, he may feel. What is so complicated about attaching a new piece of software in front of an existing system?

The problem is easier to understand if we look at the length of the development process in other areas. If we do so, we find that ten years is not an unusually long time from the first appearance of a real innovation to the point where it becomes an accepted element of current technology. That is, for example, roughly the time it took to get ovonic materials, the glassy, amorphous materials that can function as semiconductors, out of the laboratory and into commercially accepted switches and "read-mostly" memories. The ovonics example also helps make clear where the time goes. The first ovonics device, a hand-tooled "existence proof," was totally incompatible with existing semiconductor technology. Furthermore, the weight of competent opinion initially was that such a device couldn't exist. Thus a substantial amount of both technological and conceptual adaption had to occur before commercial users could be persuaded to make use of the new tool.

Computer innovations need similar adaptations. Software is not software. A given software system, like a given piece of hardware, embeds a particular conceptual structure, a set of ideas about what is worth doing and how to go about doing it. For these reasons, new software may be technologically and conceptually imcompatible with existing systems in exactly the same sense the first ovonic device was.

Thus, as the structure of decision support in the Go program is very different from that embedded in the commercially available decision support systems of today, the adaptation process, if there is one, is likely to be quite time consuming.

Another way to approach the question is to try to sketch out just what a particular adaptation might entail. For example, the Go program does strategic planning. To what extent could the underlying principles be made to serve strategic planning in a business context?

Our earlier remarks on Go and Japanese business notwithstanding, it would be hard to overestimate the differences between the world of the Go player and that of the strategic planner in business. Nonetheless, it may be helpful to have a few specific examples of the problems these differences give rise to, so that we can begin to see what might be done about them.

(A). However complex the objects and relations in Go may be, they all eventually come to the occupancy status of 361 points. The relevant objects and relations in the real world have to do with people, groups, organizations, and institutions. The Go program has its DESCRIBE component, which can derive more complex elements and relations from simpler ones, and can assess the immediate ramifications of actions in any given situation. A program for creating strategic alternatives in the real world could rely upon skilled informants for its data about actors, relations, and likely actions. But among other things, this would mean introducing error and uncertainty at the level of basic facts.

(B). In Go, every element belongs to one side or the other, and the relation between the sides is one of pure opposition: whatever one side wins, the other loses. In the real world, strict opposition occurs, but there are many more cases of opposition on some matters but not others, disagreement within a shared framework, limited cooperation, and so on. Though this introduces a layer of complexity unknown in Go, we could consider doing selective lookahead under several different goal stipulations (what happens if they go along with us on this one, and then what if they don't). We also could consider combining answers to simpler part-problems in order to approximate answers to more complex issues. This corresponds to the way complex interactions are dealt with in the Go program. PROJECT, it will be recalled, only answers individual questions. Interaction management, i.e., dealing simultaneously with several related problems, is mostly left to higher-level components.

(C). We have been treating analysis as something conducted in the service of a single interest. This may be an appropriate approximation in some cases, but in general, strategic analysis and planning often involve interactions among multiple parties. Acquisition attempts, with their multiple potential acquirers, white knights, etc., are a good illustration. Even here, however, single-interest analysis and preplanning could be a useful propaedeutic.

The foregoing discussion suggests some avenues that might be worth exploring were we determined to adapt the principles underlying the Go program for use in decision support systems for strategic planning in business. But the problems in doing so obviously are immense. Just imagine the difficulties we would have trying to ascertain the utility of such a system in the strategic planning domain. Thus, we are more or less forced to the conclusion that if we have a choice, strategic planning probably is not the best place to start. What we need is an area in which the problems are more limited and the feedback more immediate.

As one example of such an area, consider the needs of a specialist in the research department of a large futures trading firm, – Phibro for example. What kind of decision support does such an individual require? Each such specialist is likely to be responsible for a small set of related futures markets, – e.g., metals, or grains, or financial instruments. The information used falls into two broad categories: technical, and fundamental. Technical data consists of numbers (price movements, trading volumes, and changes in the numbers of outstanding contracts) generated by the trading in the market. Fundamental information includes everything directly or indirectly affecting the price of the underlying commodity. Grain fundamentals, for example, include estimates of supply and demand, weather information, interest rates (higher rates will increase the cost of holding grain), and even political factors (embargoing trade with the USSR should reduce demand for grain). Some of these factors (e.g., storm damage to sugar cane fields in the Philippines) will impact mainly one commodity; others, such as interest rate changes, may impact a whole group, or several groups at once.

Computer support for technically-based trading already is well accepted. When we turn to fundamentals, however, computerized decision support simply does not exist. There are several reasons for this. Compared with technical data, fundamental information is typically more diverse, more judgmental, more qualitative, and above all, more complexly and conditionally linked to the futures price movements we wish to predict. Take the report of an increase in the money supply, for example. Interpreting this information presumes some implicit model of seasonal changes in money supply, a model of Federal reserve intentions (are they more concerned with reducing inflation or with reducing unemployment?), and probably also some assumptions about the current psychology of the market (are traders more preoccupied about inflation, or about deflation?). The straightforward decision support models used for numerical technical data are of little help in dealing with such fundamental information.

Might the principles underlying the Go program provide a useful basis for augmenting decision support in futures trading? The problems do seem more limited than those we considered in the strategic planning case, and the feedback is certainly far more immediate and unambiguous. Furthermore, the artificial intelligence literature provides several schemes that might be used for representing and drawing inferences from the conditional, non-numeric information used in fundamental analysis. Most interesting of all, a great deal of the prognostication in futures trading involves manipulation of expectations about the actions of others (traders, producers, hedgers, political agencies, etc.) and this, of course, is just what the Go program framework is good at.

If we were to attempt this project, how would we go about it? First, we would want to be sure that we could come up with an adequate representation of the relevant facts and relations. This could be done by beginning with a single commodity or commodity group and taking an adequate sample of the causal assertions we find in advisory letters and market analyses. At some later point a representation system for such information might prove useful in ascertaining how much of the price movement variance such fundamental analyses actually can account for. At this initial stage, however, we would not need make any assumptions on this point. All we would be trying to do would be to replicate the information representation traders use, so that we could program a system to derive predictions from fundamentals as they do.

The first result of such an effort would be a system that could function as a consultant or advice-giver for the trader. That is, it would track events and update its representation, and then use the updated information to draw inferences about likely future events that might be of interest to the trader. Functioning in this mode, the system would be much closer to current conceptions of the role of decision support. For this reason, and because it would fill the fundamentals decision support gap, the system would likely stand a much greater chance of gaining acceptance as a practical tool.

11. CONCLUSION

As we have seen, constructing plausible scenarios in Go differs in many critical respects from analysis and planning in the world of business. But there are a number of important structural similarities. In both cases, the space of concrete action sequences is far too large to permit direct exhaustive search. Both presume the ability to carry one's thoughts flexibly over different levels of abstraction. Both domains also typically involve significant interactions and resource limitations, with a consequent need to discover lines of action that deal with several problems simultaneously. In both, finally, little can be accomplished without means for anticipating and taking into account the objectives of the other party or parties involved.

The success of the Go program in managing its search and decision problems in the face of these factors is attributable to the highly selective character of the search. The program limits itself to a very small number of locally good courses of action. The underlying assumption, which holds, we believe, for most human analysis in complex domains, is that if a small number of good lines come up with the same answer, then that answer very likely reflects the important determining properties of the situation being analyzed. This assumption will occasionally prove wrong, of course. Therefore, the selective lookahead processes must operate, as they do in the Go program, in the context of a general system capable of detecting and rectifying mismatches between its planning assumptions and conclusions and the emerging facts of the situation.

For the reasons sketched out in Section 10, we see no immediate prospect of using the concepts embedded in the Go program to create augmented decision support systems for strategic analysis and planning in business. Even the much simpler system for managing fundamental information for futures trading will take considerable time to develop. The ability of the Go program to selectively construct good alternatives suggests, however, that the focused multilevel search model discussed here can provide a systematic, explicit framework for examining and perhaps rationalizing strategic analysis and planning. Furthermore, as artificial intelligence develops ways of dealing with the sorts of difficulties described in Section 10, it may eventually prove feasible to create augmented decision support systems structured along the lines considered here, even for domains as complex as strategic planning in business.

NOTES AND ACKNOWLEDGMENTS

1. The approach taken here derives from the work of H.A. Simon and A. Newell, who introduced heuristics and satisfycing into programs capable of independent thinking and problem solving. The detailed framework used owes a great deal to discussions with James Kerwin, the first American to succeed in achieving professional status as a Go player. Apart from the representative search component, much of the program analysis and design, and all of the actual programming, are the work of my colleague Bruce Wilcox. Support for this work under NSF grant MCS77-0880 is gratefully acknowledged.
2. Detailed technical descriptions of the Go program have been published elsewhere (Reitman and Wilcox, 1979a, 1979b). The brief summary included here is intended only to convey a general idea of how the system works. Note that the three primary components we focus upon here (DESCRIBE, CONSTRUCT, and PROJECT) are renamed from the technical discussions published· previously, in order to facilitate this more general presentation.

REFERENCES:

[1]   Boorman, S.A., *The Protracted Game,* London: Oxford, 1969.

[2]   Broder, D.S., "Memo opens eyes," *The Ann Arbor News,* A-6, May 13, 1977.

[3]   Brown, D.J.H., and Dowsey, S., "The Challenge of Go," *New Scientist,* 81, 1979, pp. 303-305

[4]   Kerwin, J., and Reitman, W., A Go Protocol with Comments. IP-20, unpublished. University of Michigan, 1973.

[5]   Lehner, P., Planning in Adversity: A Computational Model of Strategic Planning in the Game of Go. Unpublished doctoral dissertation. University of Michigan, 1981.

[6]   Reitman, W., Nado, R., and Wilcox, B., "Machine Perception: What Makes It So Hard for Computers to See?" In C.W. Savage (ed.), *Perception and Cognition.* Minneapolis: University of Minnesota Press, 1978a, pp. 65-87.

[7]   Reitman, W., and Wilcox, B., "Pattern Recognition and Pattern-directed Inference in a Program for Playing Go." In D. Waterman and R. Hayes-Roth (Eds.), *Pattern-directed Inference Systems.* New York: Academic Press, 1978b, pp. 503-523.

[8]   Reitman, W., and Wilcox, B., "The Structure and Performance of the INTERIM.2 Go Program." Proceedings of the Sixth International Joint Conference on Artificial Intelligence, Tokyo, 1979a.

[9]   Reitman, W., and Wilcox, B., "Modeling Tactical Analysis and Problem Solving in Go." Proceedings of the Tenth Annual Pittsburgh Conference on Modelling and Simulation. Pittsburgh, 1979.

[10] Simon, H.A., "Theories of Decision-Making in Economics and Behavioral Science." *American Economic Review,* 49, 1959, pp. 253-283.